# Staying
# POSITIVE
# In A Negative
# World

## kenneth hagin jr.

# Staying
# POSITIVE
# In A Negative
# World

### kenneth hagin jr.

FAITH LIBRARY
PUBLICATIONS

Second Printing 2006
ISBN 0-89276-743-X
ISBN-13: 978-0-89276-743-4

Copyright © 2003 RHEMA Bible Church
AKA Kenneth Hagin Ministries
All Rights Reserved.
Printed in USA.

In the U.S. write:
Kenneth Hagin Ministries
P.O. Box 50126
Tulsa, OK 74150-0126
1-888-28-FAITH
www.rhema.org

In Canada write:
Kenneth Hagin Ministries
P.O. Box 335, Station D
Etobicoke (Toronto), Ontario
Canada, M9A 4X3
www.rhemacanada.org

# Contents

# Introduction

*In* a world where people are experiencing increasing fear and uncertainty about the future, the believer is commanded to walk independent of adverse circumstances, and to live by faith in the unseen — in God's eternal Word. When God's people are successful in doing so, there is a difference between them and the world, and God can move in the earth as He desires.

Christians should show forth the goodness and glory of God to a world that is hopeless, helpless, and hurting. Believers should demonstrate the riches of God's grace and kindness to those around them. Truly, it is the goodness of God that leads people to repentance (Rom. 2:4)!

I chose the subject of this book in part because of the darkness that seems to be increasing in the world today. While every generation of believers has faced dark times that have challenged their faith and tried to obscure the light of God's Word, the signs of the times point to the fact that we are living in the last of the last days.

In this book, I discuss the main factors in maintaining Christian joy and remaining positive amidst the negativity of the world. My prayer is that, through the pages of this book, you will be inspired and strengthened to hold your head up high and let your light shine for the world to see. As you do, you will be blessed, others will be blessed, and God will be glorified!

*Rev. Kenneth Hagin Jr.*

# Are You *Upbeat* or *Beat-Up*?

## one

*Christians* don't have to lie down and let life run over them. Certainly, we all experience troubles, tests, and trials at one time or another, but we serve a great God Who has made provision for us to overcome them. We simply need to know how to cooperate with Him so that He can deliver us from whatever tries to affect us negatively.

That is where many people fail to receive the blessings of God as He intended — they don't know how to cooperate with God to allow Him to move by His power on their behalf. They become weary in their faith and often give up short of receiving total victory. Weariness in faith sets the stage for total defeat.

But God wants you to stay positive in the tests and trials of life. He doesn't want you to become worn out and beat down by circumstances. Yes, circumstances are real, and they can be big. But God is bigger!

## A 'Beat-Up' Attitude Can Cause You To Forget About God

The Bible tells us of an Old Testament patriarch, who was in covenant with Almighty God, yet became weary in his faith.

**GENESIS 42:36-38**

**36 And Jacob their father said unto them, Me have ye bereaved of my children: Joseph is not, and Simeon is not, and ye will take Benjamin away: ALL THESE THINGS ARE AGAINST ME.**

**37 And Reuben spake unto his father, saying, Slay my two sons, if I bring him not to thee: deliver him into my hand, and I will bring him to thee again.**

**38 And he said, My son shall not go down with you; for his brother is dead, and he is left alone: if mischief befall him by the way in the which ye go, then shall ye bring down my gray hairs with sorrow to the grave.**

Can you relate to Jacob's feelings of helplessness and hopelessness? He said, *"All* these things are against me." I'm sure each of us has experienced problems that didn't come our way one at a time, but they came in twos, threes, and fours!

But let's look more closely at Jacob's situation.

Imagine this poor man's plight! Jacob was well advanced in age and was experiencing *multiplied* family problems. He'd lost his wife and favorite son, and another son was imprisoned in Egypt. And on top of all that, there was a famine in the land. Jacob was tired, lonely, hungry, and defeated. He began to complain.

Overwhelmed by his circumstances, he took a "beat up" attitude. He said, "Everything is against me."

This is the same man who had wrestled with the Angel of the Lord all night one night, saying, "I'm not going to let You go until You bless me" (Gen. 32:26). Jacob was a great patriarch in the land and his offspring had become the heads of the twelve tribes of Israel. Yet there he was, distressed and defeated in his mind.

Our attitude today would be like Jacob's if we began to give in to negativity and defeat, saying, "What am I going to do? How am I going to get out of this mess? God, why did You let this happen to me?" (Does that sound familiar?)

You know what I'm talking about. You've had a "beat-up" attitude — no one physically laid a hand on you, yet you felt as if you'd been "run through the wringer." You felt worn out and defeated — *beat-up!* We've *all* felt like that at one time or another.

In the midst of his trouble, Jacob forgot one thing, at least temporarily. He forgot about his God, El-Shaddai, the One Who's More Than Enough! He forgot about Jehovah Jireh, the God Who Provides!

We need to constantly remind ourselves that God is greater than any circumstance we face. He will deliver us and show us the way out of trials and adversity if we will look to Him — if we will remember Him!

I have a little placard on my desk that says, "When life gives you lemons, make lemonade." That's not just a cliché or a cute saying. That's what God wants to do in your life. He wants to take the destruction — He wants to take the bitter or sour in your life — and turn it into something sweet. He wants to reconstruct your life. But if you allow a "beat-up" attitude to control your thinking, God won't be able to move in your life like He wants to. If you wring your hands and cry, "Oh, Lord, why me?" you will hinder the power of God to turn your situation around for good. You'll lose all perspective of a positive attitude.

A "beat-up" attitude is just the attitude the enemy wants us to have. He wants us to consider the circumstances that surround us and allow those circumstances to make us feel defeated. Once we become "beat-up," he can dominate us.

## God Cares

It's understandable why Jacob had a "beat-up" attitude. He said, "All these things are against me!" And looking at his circumstances from the natural, that was a reasonable exclamation! But with God, it becomes unreasonable, because when we have a "beat-up" attitude, we underestimate not only the abilities of God, but also His love and care for us.

God cares deeply for His children and He doesn't want us to succumb to the devil's tactics. He wants to take our negative circumstances and turn them around.

The Bible says, *"Casting all your care upon him; for he careth for you"* (1 Peter 5:7). God does not want you to go through life "beat-up." He wants you to cast your cares, worries, and concerns on Him. Then straighten your shoulders, hold your head up high, and begin to rely on El Shaddai, the God Who's More Than Enough! Depend on Jehovah Jireh, the God Who Will Provide for you!

5

# A Prophet Who Went From
## *Upbeat* to *Beat-up*

Remaining positive and upbeat in a negative world is a choice you will have to make continually. If you are not mindful of God's love and power in your life, you can be "up one day and down the next," depending on the situation or circumstance.

Let's look at a couple of incidents concerning the prophet Elijah to help illustrate this point.

In First Kings 18, we read that Elijah called down fire from Heaven and then slew four hundred and fifty prophets of Baal. God used Elijah to win a mighty victory that day! Then, although there had been a severe drought over the land for more than two years, Elijah prayed to God, and the sky began to turn black as the rain clouds formed and the winds began to blow. Afterward, a great rain came, and the Spirit of God came on Elijah and enabled him to outrun King Ahab's chariot — all the way to the city of Jezreel!

Then in First Kings 19:1, Ahab reported to Queen Jezebel that Elijah had killed all the prophets of Baal. Jezebel sent a messenger to Elijah to tell him, *". . . So let the gods do to me, and more also, if I make not thy life*

*as the life of one of them by to morrow about this time"*
(v. 2).

Let's look at some other verses in this chapter to see
what this mighty man, Elijah, did when he heard the
news that Jezebel intended to kill him.

**1  KINGS 19:3,4**
**3  And when he saw that, he arose, and
went for his life, and came to Beersheba,
which belongeth to Judah, and left his ser-
vant there.
4  But he himself went a day's journey into
the wilderness, and came and sat down
under a juniper tree: and he requested for
himself that he might die; and said, It is
enough; now, O Lord, take away my life; for I
am not better than my fathers.**

Once day, Elijah was performing exploits and wonders by the Spirit of God, and the next day, he was running for his life! He went from being *upbeat* to *beat-up!*
After forty days, Elijah came to Horeb and entered a
cave (vv. 5-8). The Lord said to him, "What are you
doing!" (v. 9.) Or we might say the Lord said to him,
"What's the matter with you!"

Elijah cried, *". . . the children of Israel have forsaken thy covenant, thrown down thine altars, and slain thy prophets with the sword; and I, even I only, am left; and they seek my life, to take it away"* (v. 10). Elijah was complaining, "I'm the only one serving You; I'm the only one left."

In verse 13, God asked Elijah again, *". . . What doest thou here, Elijah?"* Then in verse 18, God said, *". . . I have left me seven thousand in Israel, all the knees which have not bowed unto Baal, and every mouth which hath not kissed him."* In other words, God was saying, "No, Elijah, you're *not* the only one left."

What the enemy wants to do to us today is to get us to think we're "the only one left" — or we're the only one facing *this* kind of test or trial.

But you're not the only one! First Peter 5:8-9 proves that, saying, *"Be sober, be vigilant; because your adversary the devil, as a roaring lion, walketh about, seeking whom he may devour: Whom resist stedfast in the faith, KNOWING THAT THE SAME AFFLICTIONS ARE ACCOMPLISHED IN YOUR BRETHREN that are in the world."*

You're not the only one who's going through whatever kind of test or trial you are facing. We all face tests and trials. And we each must make a decision about our attitude. Will we be *upbeat* or *beat-up?*

# A Lesson From Paul

The Apostle Paul met great challenges too. But in contrast to Jacob's attitude, the Apostle Paul made a faith stand in the face of adversity.

**ROMANS 8:37**
**37 Nay, IN ALL THESE THINGS we are more than conquerors through him that loved us.**

Notice the difference in the attitudes of these two men: Jacob said, "All these things are against me. I've had it!" Paul said, "Yet *in* all these things, I am *more than a conqueror!*"

It seems that Jacob forgot about God as El Shaddai and Jehovah Jireh. Paul, on the other hand, focused on God and His greatness. Jacob forgot that God was bigger than all of his trouble; Paul considered the power of God. Jacob forgot that God loved and cared about him; Paul was very conscious of God's loving care.

Someone said, "Yes, but Paul was a great apostle!"

Nevertheless, Paul knew what it was to experience suffering and hardship. Let's look at how bad it was for him.

**2 CORINTHIANS 11:23-28 (*NIV*)**
**23 Are they servants of Christ? (I am out of my mind to talk like this.) I am more. I have**

worked much harder, been in prison more frequently, been flogged more severely, and been exposed to death again and again.

24 Five times I received from the Jews the forty lashes minus one.

25 Three times I was beaten with rods, once I was stoned, three times I was shipwrecked, I spent a night and a day in the open sea,

26 I have been constantly on the move. I have been in danger from rivers, in danger from bandits, in danger from my own countrymen, in danger from Gentiles; in danger in the city, in danger in the country, in danger at sea; and in danger from false brothers.

27 I have laboured and toiled and have often gone without sleep; I have known hunger and thirst and often gone without food; I have been cold and naked.

28 Besides everything else, I face daily the pressure of my concern for all the churches.

Here Paul enumerated his hardships and toils — he didn't deny the existence of his problems. But you see, it's one thing when you have troubles; it's another thing entirely when troubles have *you!*

## The Power of Choice

When you have a "beat-up" attitude, troubles have you. But in the midst of troubles, you can take a lesson from Paul and be upbeat, or you can respond as Jacob did, saying, "All these things are against me."

I once read something very interesting that a World War II Holocaust survivor said along this line. He said, "The last of the human freedoms is to choose one's attitude in any given set of circumstances."

You see, it's our choice what kind of attitude we take in the tests and trials of life. It's up to us what attitude we demonstrate when people talk against us or lie about us. A negative attitude will not only dampen our spirit and weaken us, but it will hinder the power of God from working in our life. A "beat-up" attitude will cause us to want to give up and quit — to give up our will to succeed.

But with faith in God, an upbeat attitude will buoy up our spirit and keep us strong through the storms of life so that we can walk in victory. An upbeat attitude can help us to rise up and face our challenge with confidence. We *can* walk out triumphantly on the other side of our test, if we'll make a stand with God.

# It Takes Commitment

## two

*It's* sad to say, but far too many Christians live burdened down by the negative influence of the world. They accept failure too readily, because they have allowed their faith to become weak and their spirit to grow faint from the negativity around them.

Of course, it would be foolish to deny that we live in a negative world. We live in a world full of trouble. *Real* problems exist everywhere. And if existing problems are not bad enough, we constantly face predictions of *impending* natural, economic, and political disasters — everything from the fall of major governments to the burning of the planet due to a depleted ozone!

So what is a Christian supposed to do?

First, we can take comfort in the fact that nothing in the world today is news to God; nothing is taking Him by surprise. In fact, He warned us about our difficulties in John 16:33, *". . . In this world you will have trouble . . ."* (*NIV*).

Now these are the words of Jesus! He said trouble is sure to come — but that's not all He said. He added these encouraging words: *"These things I have spoken unto you, that in me ye might have peace. In the world ye shall have tribulation: BUT BE OF GOOD CHEER; I have overcome the world"* (John 16:33).

Jesus told us in this verse to take heart — to be of good cheer — in the midst of storms. Yet instead of having a cheerful attitude, Christians often become negative. They complain until they become as weary, hopeless, and negative as the world around them.

In the natural, because of all of the trouble in the world, we have smart bombs, home security systems, law enforcement agencies, prisons, hospitals, medical personnel, and so forth to "help" us feel at peace. But despite all of man's assistance, people are still fearful and crying out for help. Many of them are grasping for hope, yet at the same time, saying, "What are we going to do? It's hopeless. We can't win."

So the question of the day might be this: *Is it really possible to remain positive in such a negative environment — when things look so bad around us?*

Let's go to the Bible to answer that question.

## They Refused To Bow

Throughout the Bible, we read of those who "kept the faith" and refused to be influenced by the darkness and negativity that surrounded them. Three such men were Shadrach, Meshach, and Abednego.

These three young Hebrew men were living in exile, serving as administrators over the province of Babylon under King Nebuchadnezzar. The three men enjoyed God's favor, even in captivity. Everything seemed to be going great for them until one day when a decree went out from the king: At a certain time, when the music played, the entire province had to bow and worship the king's golden image!

When the time came and the music began, Shadrach, Meshach, and Abednego refused to pay homage to the golden image. The penalty for such rebellion was to be thrown into a fiery furnace!

The king, who had been favorably disposed toward the three men, became angry, yet gave them a second chance to bow to his image. He said, *"Now if ye be ready that at what time ye hear the sound . . . ye fall down and worship the image which I have made; well: but if ye worship not, ye shall be cast the same hour into the midst of a burning fiery furnace; and who is that God that shall deliver you out of my hands?"* (Dan. 3:15).

But Shadrach, Meshach, and Abednego still would not bow!

> **DANIEL 3:16-18**
> **16 Shadrach, Meshach, and Abednego, answered and said to the king, O Nebuchadnezzar, we are not careful to answer thee in this matter.**
> **17 If it be so, our God whom we serve is able to deliver us from the burning fiery furnace, and he will deliver us out of thine hand, O king.**
> **18 But if not, be it known unto thee, O king, that we will not serve thy gods, nor worship the golden image which thou hast set up.**

People debate about verse 18, some saying that the three Hebrew men were unsure or unsteady about their faith in God's willingness to deliver them. They say, "First the three were in faith, saying, 'God will deliver us.' Then they got out of faith, saying, 'But if He *doesn't . . . .'"*

Others disagree, saying that the Hebrew men said, "O king, God will deliver us. But even if you *don't* throw us in the furnace, we still will not worship the image."

I believe Shadrach, Meshach, and Abednego's strong commitment to God and His Word strengthened their resolve not to worship that image — even *if* the burning furnace awaited them. Their *faith* said God would deliver them; their *commitment* said it didn't make any difference whether He did or didn't — they were not going to worship the king's golden image!

*Things really looked bad, but it was settled — they would not bow!*

## A Strong Commitment *to* God Brings Strong Confidence *in* God!

Simply put, Shadrach, Meshach, and Abednego's *faith* spoke in verse 17; their *commitment* spoke in verse 18. They proclaimed: "Even if God doesn't deliver us, we are going to stand true to Him. We are going to stand true to His Word. We are *not* going to worship other gods."

This verbal response to the king had nothing to do with a lack of faith, but it had everything to do with a total commitment to do the right thing in honor of the One they served. Their strong commitment produced in

them a strong confidence that He would deliver them —
and God did exactly that.

At their continued defiance, the king became so furi-
ous that he had the furnace heated seven times hotter
than usual. The intense heat, meant to destroy the
young Hebrew men, overcame and killed the men who
cast them, bound, into the fire!

Later the surprised and bewildered king, looking
into the furnace, asked his advisors, "Didn't we cast
three men, *bound,* into the fire?"

"Yes, three men," they answered.

"Well, I see four men, *loose,* walking around in the
fire! They're not hurt, and the Fourth Man is like the
Son of God!"

King Nebuchadnezzar called Shadrach, Meshach,
and Abednego out of the fire, and when they came
forth, not a single hair was singed, their clothing wasn't
damaged, and they didn't even *smell* like smoke! The
Bible says that the people gathered to see these three
men *". . . upon whose bodies the fire had no power!"*
(Dan. 3:27).

You see, we must be committed to God and His
Word to successfully walk this walk of faith in the face
of negative circumstances. Walking by faith is not something we just "try." No, we must take hold of God's

Word like a dog with a bone! We must have the attitude,
"Sink or swim, I'm going to believe God. No matter
what bad circumstance is going on around me, I will not
give in!"

## Faith, Commitment, and a Den of Lions

This level of commitment to God and His Word is a
big part of faith that we perhaps haven't seen as clearly
as we should. But we need to realize that God honors
steadfast faith.

Let's look at another report of commitment found in
the Bible.

During the reign of King Darius of Babylon, Daniel
was placed as one of three rulers (or presidents) over
120 princes who officiated over the entire province. Of
the three main rulers under the king, Daniel was favored,
". . . *because an excellent spirit was in him; and the king
thought to set him over the whole realm*" (Dan. 6:3).

The other two presidents and the 120 princes were
jealous of Daniel, and sought to find something to use
against him before the king. But they could find no
fault in him because he was faithful to the king and
without error in the administration of his duties. So they
plotted against Daniel and tricked the king into signing
a decree that contradicted the law of Daniel's God. The

decree said, for thirty days, anyone who prayed or made petition to any god but the king would be cast into a den of lions.

So what did Daniel do when he discovered that the decree had been established and the proclamation made? He went into his house, and *with the windows open*, he prayed to his God (Dan. 6:10)!

The men who had conspired against Daniel wasted no time telling the king what Daniel had done. But King Darius, distraught because he favored Daniel, looked for a way to deliver Daniel from his impending execution. Yet the decree was written "according to the law of the Medes and Persians," which meant it could not be changed (Dan. 6:8,12,15).

So the king commanded his servants to throw Daniel into the den of lions. But notice what Darius said to Daniel: "*. . . Thy God whom thou servest continually, he will deliver thee*" (v. 16)!

**DANIEL 6:18-23**
**18 Then the king went to his palace, and passed the night fasting: neither were instruments of musick brought before him: and his sleep went from him.**

**19 Then the king arose very early in the
morning, and went in haste unto the den of
lions.**

**20 And when he came to the den, he cried
with a lamentable voice unto Daniel: and the
king spake and said to Daniel, O Daniel, ser-
vant of the living God, is thy God, whom
thou servest continually, able to deliver thee
from the lions?**

**21 Then said Daniel unto the king, O king,
live for ever.**

**22 My God hath sent his angel, and hath
shut the lions' mouths, that they have not
hurt me: forasmuch as before him innocency
was found in me; and also before thee, O
king, have I done no hurt.**

**23 Then was the king exceeding glad for
him, and commanded that they should take
Daniel up out of the den . . . and no manner
of hurt was found upon him, because he
believed in his God.**

Why did Daniel have such confidence in his God
while facing this life-threatening circumstance? Because
he served God *continually* (vv. 16,20). He knew God.

Daniel's faith for deliverance was born out of his commitment to God. And because of his attitude, Daniel had favor with God — the lions didn't harm a hair on Daniel's head!

Now let's read verse 24 to find out what happened to those who plotted against Daniel. The king commanded his servants to throw them into the same den of lions, along with their families. And the Bible says, *". . . the lions had the mastery of them . . ."* and killed them all.

This story shows that it pays to stay committed to God. Serving God continually can change things for us; we can be spared in the midst of trouble too. Despite any disaster that comes against us, we can come out unscathed if, like Daniel, we stand for God, believing He is willing and able to protect us.

# God Is Able!

From the pages of the Word of God, we continually hear the voices of men and women of God raising up a cry, "God is able!" They were tested and tried, yet like Daniel, Shadrach, Meshach, and Abednego, they would not give in. Although they were pressed by trouble on every side, they made a decision to never allow the pressure to alter their faith in God's ability to protect and save them.

If we could ask Abraham, David, Moses, Joshua, Paul, Peter, and John if God is indeed able, we'd hear them answer with one voice, rising in crescendo, *"Yes! Our God is able!"* And Sarah, Hannah, Ruth, Deborah, and Mary would also join in the proclamation, singing the song of the Ages: "Our God is able!"

We need to make the same declaration, exalting the Name of our God and the power of God over all the darkness and negativism the world tries to bring. We should continually proclaim, "Our God is able!"

Some people in the world have the attitude (and this attitude has gotten over into the Church), "You can't win them all. You have to take the good with the bad. You have to accept some defeat. So why not be satisfied with your lot in life?"

But there is a way to live a positive lifestyle in God — an overcoming, victorious lifestyle! The Bible says, *". . . all things are possible to him that believeth"* (Mark 9:23). The Lord has made provision for us to live above and beyond any adverse circumstances that may surround us.

# God Wants To Answer Your Prayers!

## three

*The* world needs a positive influence from Christians. Jesus said in Matthew 5:16, *"Let your light so shine before men, that they may see your good works, and glorify your Father which is in heaven."*

It's important to know that a positive influence glorifies our Father in Heaven! And if we are going to *stay* positive, we need to commit ourselves to prayer.

We must never underestimate the importance of prayer in maintaining a level of peace when we are surrounded by negativity. Philippians 4:6,7 *says, "Do not be anxious about anything, but in everything, by prayer and petition, with thanksgiving, present your requests to God. And the peace of God, which transcends all understanding, will guard your hearts and your minds in Christ Jesus"* (NIV).

25

In this passage, Paul tells us to present our problems to God instead of worrying about them — *then* God's peace will come into our heart and mind.

## The Negative Force of Worry

We must resist the temptation to worry. Why? Because *God* told us not to be anxious about *anything.*

We were not designed to carry anxiety and burdens. Yet if we're not careful, we can allow our minds to become disappointed, discouraged, and depressed. We can allow worry to enter in instead of what God has said.

Worry is designed to distract you from the Word of God. The devil tries to get us to spend our time worrying about things — and, often, about things that haven't happened yet and probably *never will* happen. If he is successful, we will become more and more negative, and our faith and prayer life will be ineffective.

Friend, God wants to answer your prayers! He wants you to bring your concerns to Him — to cast your anxiety on Him. First Peter 5:7 says, *"Cast all your anxiety [worry, care] on him because he cares for you"* (NIV).

## The Power of Prayer

John Wesley, the eighteenth-century founder of Methodism, once said, "It seems God is limited by our prayer life — that He can do nothing for humanity unless someone asks Him."

In Mark 11:24, Jesus Himself said, *"Therefore I tell you, whatever you ask for in prayer, believe that you have received it, and it will be yours"* (NIV).

And consider what Jesus said about prayer in the following verses:

**JOHN 14:13,14**

**13 And whatsoever ye shall ask in my name, that will I do, that the Father may be glorified in the Son.**

**14 If ye shall ask any thing in my name, I will do it.**

**JOHN 15:7,8**

**7  If ye abide in me, and my words abide in you, ye shall ask what ye will, and it shall be done unto you.**

**8  Herein is my Father glorified, that ye bear much fruit.**

The fruit Jesus spoke about in verse 8 is *answered prayer*. God gets the glory when we receive answers to prayer! And answered prayer is one of God's greatest blessings to enable us to remain in peace — to maintain a positive attitude.

Remember, Philippians 4:6 says, *"Do not be anxious about anything, but in everything, by prayer and petition, with thanksgiving, present your requests to God"* (*NIV*). When we pray, we give Him not only our petitions, but also our burdens. In exchange, He gives us His peace that passes our human understanding and the promise that He will take care of us and answer our prayers. He relieves us of the anxiety, worry, and care associated with our problem so that we can stay positive and thank Him for the answer, while we are expecting it to come to pass!

## Your Requests Can Become Realities

Praying in faith will bring you into victory on the other side of every test or trial. On the other side of every sickness, disease, financial problem, or whatever you're facing — victory awaits you!

The following verses support that truth:

**HEBREWS 4:16**

**16 Let us therefore come boldly unto the throne of grace, that we may obtain mercy, and find grace to help in time of need.**

**HEBREWS 10:23,35**

**23 Let us hold fast the profession of our faith without wavering; (for he is faithful that promised). . . .**

**35 Cast not away therefore your confidence, which hath great recompense of reward.**

The Bible patriarchs of old, who won tremendous victories in prayer, practiced these verses before they were ever written! They brought their requests to God boldly, obtaining mercy and grace from Him in their time of need. They judged Him faithful and held on to their confidence and godly hope until they saw their answer come.

Modern-day patriarchs in the faith have also proved God's faithfulness to answer prayer. Let's look at one of them.

## George Mueller of Bristol

In the nineteenth century, George Mueller founded a great chain of orphanages on nothing but prayer. He lived by faith, refusing to inform anyone of his needs. Instead, he mentioned them only to God on his knees in prayer. At one point in his ministry, he housed more than 10,000 orphans with no steady financial resource. He trusted God daily to meet their needs.

Rev. Mueller estimated God "had answered over 50,000 of his prayers, many thousands of which were answered on the day he made them and often before he arose from his knees."[1] His fruitful prayer life can be traced back to his commitment to the Word of God. He read the Bible through 200 times in his lifetime, 100 of those times while on his knees before God.[2]

Rev. Mueller wrote the following poem concerning prayer:

> I believe God answers prayer,
> Answers always, everywhere;
> I may cast my anxious care,
> Burdens I could never bear,
> On the God who heareth prayer.
> Never need my soul despair
> Since He bids me boldly dare
> To the secret place repair,
> There to prove He answers prayer.[3]

George Mueller performed exploits for God in his ministry to orphaned children. At times, there wasn't a morsel of food in the entire orphanage for hundreds of children. But Mueller and his staff would pray. Again and again, he records "money or supplies had arrived with only minutes to spare before the children sat down at the table."[4] Why do you think he (and others like him) could make such an impact on mankind? Because he was saturated with the Word and had a strong faith and confidence in his prayer-answering God!

## The Effects of Prayer on a Nation

In Second Chronicles 7:14, God told Israel, "If my people, which are called by my name, shall humble themselves, and pray, and seek my face, and turn from their wicked ways; then will I hear from heaven, and will forgive their sin, and will heal their land."

This is no less true for us today. Considering the unprecedented decisions made every day, we should pray for our nation and for those in authority on every level — national, state, and local.

The apostle Paul said, *"I exhort therefore, that, first of all, supplications, prayers, intercessions, and giving of thanks, be made for all men; For kings, and for all that*

*are in authority; that we may lead a quiet and peace-*
*able life in all godliness and honesty"* (1 Tim. 2:1,2).

Far too often, Christians fail to pray for those in
authority — those who make decisions that affect all
our lives — yet Paul says to do it *first* when we pray!
Many don't fully comprehend the huge benefit that
comes from such obedience: a *quiet and peaceable* life!

We must not neglect this important matter of prayer.
We need to believe that God wants to answer our
prayers, and then do something about it — we must
pray!

---

[1] Basil Miller, *George Mueller Man of Faith and Miracle* (Minneapolis: Bethany House Publishers, 1941), pp. 22, 145.

[2] Ibid., p. 142.

[3] Arthur T. Pierson, *George Mueller of Bristol* (Old Tappan: Revell, not indicated), p. 153.

[4] George Mueller, *Delighted in God* (Roger Steer Harold Shaw Publishers, 1981), p. 109.

# Where We're Missing It

*We* have looked at Philippians 4:6 concerning prayer: *"Be careful [or anxious] for nothing; but in every thing by prayer and supplication with thanksgiving let your requests be made known unto God."*

In this verse, God not only told us to pray or make requests, He told us how to do it — *with thanksgiving!*

The Church has spent far too little time studying thanksgiving and praise.[1] I say that because God once showed me that many Christians aren't missing it so much in their faith walk or their love walk, but they are missing it in their *praise.* We have underestimated the tremendous power that is available when we praise God.

The Bible emphasizes the power of prayer and praise in this story:

**ACTS 16:25,26**

**25 And at midnight Paul and Silas PRAYED, and SANG PRAISES unto God: and the prisoners heard them.**

**26 And suddenly there was a great earthquake, so that the foundations of the prison were shaken: and immediately all the doors were opened, and every one's bands were loosed.**

Paul and Silas had been imprisoned for preaching the Gospel. They had been placed in the very deepest, darkest part of the prison — the inner prison, in a dungeon. They had been beaten, their backs were bleeding, and their feet were bound in stocks (Acts 16:23,24). Yet they prayed and sang praises — and their deliverance came!

Paul and Silas' experience helps us see the benefits of praising God. It helps us see that to live above negative circumstances, we must pray and praise.

No matter what adverse circumstance shows up, we can experience the victory that God intends for us. But just as Paul and Silas did, we'll have to hold fast to the following three points about praise:

### 1. Don't Panic!

When life's difficult situations come, *don't panic!* Praise instead.

You may be thinking, *"It's easy to praise God when everything's going great, but things don't always go right! Things don't always go our way or according to plans. So how do we praise when things are not going right?"*

A Christian can view trouble and problems from Jesus' perspective: *He has overcome the world* — and He did it for us! If we will get hold of that truth and act on it, we can resist the urge to panic. We can "be of good cheer," by yielding to God in praise.

I imagine Paul and Silas had to fight the urge to panic when they found themselves locked up in that dark prison. The devil was no different then than he is today. I'm sure he said negative things to them, such as, "It's all over for you guys. They're going to take you out of here in the morning and put you six feet under. You'll never make it out of here alive."

Imagine for a moment what it was like in that prison cell. Picture in your mind the four walls seeming to close in on these two men. Imagine the thick, damp darkness and the stench of human waste that surrounded them.

Listen to the groaning of the other prisoners who had also been beaten.

I'm sure Paul and Silas didn't *feel* like being of good cheer! I'm sure they didn't *feel* like praising the Lord. There they sat, imprisoned and bound — in excruciating pain — with no natural hope of escape. But we see that Paul and Silas emerged victorious from their circumstances — they tapped into the supernatural power of God, and they did it through praise.

## Victory or Defeat?

We may not be in a literal prison today, but circumstances can arise that cause us to feel bound. Health problems, financial problems, and family problems can seem to close in on us. Or maybe we find ourselves having to deal with false accusations, betrayal, and senseless conflict. All of these can cause us to panic if we don't keep our guard up.

As long as we're alive on this earth, we will experience trouble and problems at some time or another. How we react to them will determine whether we have victory or defeat. Yielding to panic and fear will only add to our trouble. Panic will magnify the problem until it becomes even bigger in our eyes than it really is.

The devil loves to get us into a negative situation and then try to make us think the problem is bigger than it really is. Many times, we panic, not because of the problem, but because of our own thinking. And sometimes we panic when the problem doesn't even exist — and probably *won't* ever exist. But yielding to fear robs us of our faith, our joy, and our peace.

Now I'm not making light of problems. Real problems do arise and do exist in our lives. But panic is never the proper response to them. Praise is the key to victory.

We can yield to praise fully persuaded that God loves us no matter what we may be going through — no matter how we got there. God wants to deliver us *because* He loves us. He wants us to remain positive and to shine as lights in a dark, negative world.

## Love's Power

Nothing you are going through can diminish God's love for you. And if you will rely on His Word about His love, you will begin to praise Him, and you will find deliverance.

In God's love is the power to overcome!

**ROMANS 8:35,37-39 (*NIV*)**

**35 Who shall separate us from the love of Christ? Shall trouble or hardship or persecution or famine or nakedness or danger or sword?**

**37 No, in all these things we are more than conquerors through him who loved us.**

**38 For I am convinced that neither death nor life, neither angels nor demons, neither the present nor the future, nor any powers,**

**39 neither height nor depth, nor anything else in all creation, will be able to separate us from the love of God that is in Christ Jesus our Lord.**

Whatever trouble or hardship you face — sickness, lack of money, persecution, conflict in relationships, and so forth — "in all these things" we are not just conquerors, but we are *more* than conquerors!

**ROMANS 8:32 (*NIV*)**

**32 He who did not spare his own Son, but gave him up for us all — how will he not also, along with him, graciously give us all things?**

Since God did not spare His own Son who died on the Cross of Calvary, do you think He would withhold any other good thing from us? No — a thousand times, no! God went so far as to give His only begotten Son (John 3:16) for our restoration and deliverance, so you can rest assured that He wants to deliver you out of your tests and trials!

So don't panic! *Don't ever panic.* God will see you through.

Now let's consider our next point concerning praise:

### 2. Don't Be Problem-Conscious

So often people focus on the imperfections of life. They focus on the negative instead of the positive — on what they *don't* have instead of what they *do* have.

No one is exempt from problems, but we don't have to dwell on them. This world is not perfect, and people are not perfect. The only perfect One to live on this earth was crucified on the Cross. But thank God for Jesus' perfection, because it is through his perfection that we have life "more abundantly" (John 10:10). It is through His death, burial, and resurrection that we have been delivered and set free from the chains of sin, sickness, and disease. It is through His perfection that we have a promise of a positive future.

## It Is a Question of Focus

You don't have to let the problems of life distract you from the goodness of God. A test or trial is not worth being separated from the power of God. When we fail to pray and to praise Him, we allow negativism to shroud our faith, causing us to lose focus on God and His Word.

But the point is, nothing can separate you from God unless *you* allow it! We don't have to focus on imperfections and problems. Instead, we can focus on God's perfection.

*Our imperfections fade from our consciousness when we gaze at His perfection.* Years ago, there was a popular song entitled "Turn Your Eyes Upon Jesus." The song went like this: "Turn your eyes upon Jesus. Look full in His wonderful face. And the things of earth will grow strangely dim, In the light of His glory and grace."

You can't look to Jesus and remain focused on all the problems going on around you. When you begin to focus on Him and His power, everything else grows dim in comparison.

You see, it's a question of focus. We should focus on redemption, not on destruction, and on deliverance, not on bondage. We should focus on joy, not on sorrow and unhappiness, and on peace, not on confusion.

I ministered a message along this line, and the Lord gave me the following word of exhortation for the people:

I am He Who sits On High. And I am He Who will deliver you and bring you through to great victory. So get your focus on Me, and quit looking to the right and to the left. Look to Me and I will bring you through, and you will have great cause to rejoice and shout, because your focus is on Me and not on the problem.

Do you know why we get "stuck in the mud" in our faith and why we "spin our wheels" at times? Because we take our focus off God. We lose sight of the fact that God is bigger than our problem, and that He can deliver us. *He is able!* Yet how often in the midst of a problem do we start wringing our hands and saying, "Oh, God, what are we going to do now?"

When you're faced with a test or trial, it would help you to say out loud, "God is bigger than my problem!" If you get hold of that simple truth, it will change your focus from your problem to your answer and from the negative to the positive according to God's Word.

Paul and Silas began praising God, and it helped them remain God-conscious instead of problem-conscious. And when you find yourself in the midst of a storm or bound in a prison of circumstances, you need to keep yourself conscious of God. If not, you will become problem-conscious and defeat-conscious.

# Deliverance Is Coming!

The best thing you can do when overcoming the devil and the problems he brings your way is to keep the Word ever before you. Quote it and praise God continually for His Word. Listen to good Christian music — especially songs written about the deliverance available through the precious blood of the Jesus.

Our deliverance is in the blood of the Lamb of God. The Bible says that without the shedding of blood, there is no remission of sin (Heb. 9:22). As far as God was concerned, one final Lamb was slain on the Cross. Up until the time of Jesus' crucifixion, many lambs had been slain as atonement for the people's sins. Every year, the Jews had to slay a lamb as a sacrifice for sin.

But Jesus Christ, "the Lamb of God slain from the foundation of the world" (Rev. 13:8), shed His blood on Golgotha's hill. We don't need any other blood to be shed for remission of sin. All we need to do is to believe on the Lord Jesus Christ and confess Him as our Savior and Lord, and we are delivered from sin. We enter into the redemption He wrought for us. There's nothing more positive than having a revelation of the plan of redemption. Jesus is worthy of our praise!

Friend, that means, in Christ, you're free! The devil may think he has you bound — and at times, *you* may think he has you bound — but you are free! You can praise God and trust *Him* with your problem.

Now let's find out more about praising God.

### 3. Don't Be a Pessimist!

We've discovered two points to help us stay in an attitude of praise. First, it's better to praise than panic; and second, it's better to praise than become problem-conscious. My final point about praise is: *it's better to praise than be pessimistic.*

Have you ever met a pessimist? To a pessimist, everything has a bad side. A pessimist doesn't expect good things to happen to him or her. It's just a joke, but it's been said that if you need to borrow money, borrow it from a pessimist, because he doesn't expect you to pay him back!

Now I said that was a joke. Of course you're supposed to repay your debts, no matter whom you owe.

But my point is, a pessimist always looks at everything negatively and expects the worst.

The truth is, you can't keep your focus on God and expect the worst! When you begin focusing on God and His Word, and talking about the things of God, about His power and goodness, your outlook will change.

It seems that some people are natural grumblers and complainers. They find fault with everything. They gripe by choice. Over time, they have become cynical and pessimistic. They don't experience any of the glory and power of God, because they don't *expect* any of His glory or power.

Paul and Silas could have easily become cynical and pessimistic in that prison cell. They could have lost their focus and become bitter against God and against other people. They could have doubted God's love for them — His willingness and His ability to deliver them. They could have said, "God, why did You let this happen? We were serving You. We were preaching the Gospel for You."

But they didn't! In their midnight hour, their darkest hour, they lifted their voices and prayed and sang praises to God. They didn't give place to panic, to problems, *or* to pessimism!

## Pessimism: Doubt in Action

Paul and Silas could have blamed each other. (A pessimist will almost always try to blame someone else for his or her problems.) Silas could have said something to this effect, "Paul, you got me into this mess. This trip was your idea, and you talked me in to coming along."

Paul could have said, "Well, Silas, if you had been standing guard like you were supposed to, you would have known they were coming, and we could have escaped."

If Paul and Silas had blamed each other, it would have caused division. You see, pessimism gives place to the devil. And when you give place to the devil, he will always try to bring something else into the equation to keep you bound in darkness.

Pessimism is the opposite of faith; *it is doubt in action!* The pessimist has the attitude, "I don't really believe God will do it." But the person who walks by faith says, "I believe God can and will do it for me! I believe I receive my answer. It's mine; I have it now." You simply can't exercise faith and be pessimistic at the same time!

## The Greatest Reason To Be Optimistic

Christians have every reason to be optimistic; the Bible says God is on our side! For instance, Romans 8:31 says, *". . . If God is for us, who can be against us"* (*NIV*)? Glory! Friend, we have every reason to praise the Lord — because we know He is on our side! Praise Him for that! Praise will bring God's power on the scene to bring us through *every* trial, no matter how dark or stormy.

Let's look again at Philippians 4:6-8.

**PHILIPPIANS 4:6-8 (*NIV*)**

**6  Do not be anxious about anything, but in everything, by prayer and petition, with thanksgiving, present your requests to God.**

**7  And the peace of God, which transcends all understanding, will guard your hearts and your minds in Christ Jesus.**

**8  Finally, brothers, whatever is true, whatever is noble, whatever is right, whatever is pure, whatever is lovely, whatever is admirable — if anything is excellent or praiseworthy — think about such things.**

Verse 7 says that when we pray in faith and confidence according to His Word, He promises to guard, or garrison, our hearts and minds with His peace. That supernatural peace grounds us so that we won't give way to panic and fear.

Verse 8 tells us how to focus on the answer, not on the problem, and how to prevail over pessimism — by thinking only on good, positive things.

Praising God is a powerful thing, because it demonstrates your faith and allows God to show Himself strong on your behalf. Praising God opens the door for His blessings to fall on you. It gives you an avenue of witness — praise is contagious. When you continually praise God, others will want to know how you can have such a joyful attitude in the midst of problems, tests, and trials. They will want to know how they, too, can stay positive in a negative world.

----

[1] For an in-depth study on the subject, *see* Rev. Hagin Jr.'s book *The Untapped Power of Praise*.

# The Positive Force of Gratitude

## five

*The* Bible says that every good and perfect gift —
every good thing — comes from God (James 1:17).
When we come to realize that, we have a higher level
of consciousness of God's love. And every time we
specifically count our blessings, we come to a higher
level of praise.

Even when circumstances are negative, we can find
something positive to thank God for. I have practiced
this habit of thanksgiving all of my life. For example,
every time I participate in a softball or basketball game,
before each game, I'll say, "Thank You, Lord, that I
have a well body. Thank You that I can run. Thank You
that I can throw a ball and enjoy sports. Thank You,
Lord for strong arms and legs and for lungs that can
breathe deeply."

Every time I drive into my driveway at home, I raise my hand and breathe a prayer to God, "Thank You for this house. It's my haven. It's a refuge and place of rest and refreshing for Lynette and me. Thank You, Father." And, of course, I continually thank God for the wife, children, and grandchildren He has given me, and for the fact that they're all healthy and strong.

It is so important to thank God for the blessings we have, instead of complaining about what we don't have. I have found that when we're thankful for what we already have, God gives us more. But when we murmur, gripe, and complain, we put ourselves in a position of doubt and unbelief. We cross over the fence, so to speak, from being positive to being negative, and God can't bless us when we're in that position. He *wants* to bless us, but He can't; we've taken ourselves out of position to receive from Him.

A. W. Tozer, a twentieth-century minister and theologian, said, "Thanksgiving has creative power!"

It's true. Our attitude of thanksgiving to God not only strengthens our faith and inspires those around us; our praise also blesses the Father. The Bible says He inhabits the praises of His people (Ps. 22:3). In the Old Testament, the Israelites were known as the "people of God." And in the New Testament, we who have been born again are His people too. We are His children, and He is our very own Father Who inhabits our praises!

## From a Parent's Point of View

If you are a parent, you know the feelings you experience when your children are truly thankful for something you've done for them. You naturally desire to bless your children and to meet their needs. But when they thank you for the things you do for them, and show genuine gratitude, you feel even more determined to do whatever you can to bless and benefit them. You feel great about giving even more good things to them.

We have that attitude as parents because that is our Heavenly Father's attitude toward us. Matthew 7:11 says, *"If ye then, being evil* [or natural], *know how to give good gifts unto your children, how much more shall your Father which is in heaven give good things to them that ask him?"* How much more do you think *God* is inclined to bestow blessings when we enter His Presence just to thank Him for His benefits and for the blessings we've already received?

Sometimes, we should enter His Presence just to say, "Father, I come not to ask anything, but just to worship You and thank You for what You have done for me."

Being grateful is a form of praise. In the natural, we enjoy giving things to people who are grateful. God is the same way.

# Count Your Blessings

When I was a kid, there was a certain song we sang in church called, "Count Your Blessings." The lyrics said: "Count your blessings; name them one by one. Count your blessings; see what God hath done." It was a good song.

We need to continually count our blessings, stirring ourselves up to remember the benefits God has provided for us. Let's look at the words of the psalmist David, who saw this important truth in his own life.

**PSALM 103:1-5 (*NIV*)**

**1   Praise the Lord, O my soul; all my inmost being, praise his holy name.**

**2   Praise the Lord, O my soul, and forget not all his benefits —**

**3   who forgives all your sins and heals all your diseases,**

**4   who redeems your life from the pit and crowns you with love and compassion,**

**5  who satisfies your desires with good
things so that your youth is renewed like the
eagle's.**

Some people read this passage and say, "Oh, what
nice verses. And the words make such a nice song."
Well, the entire book of Psalms was written as a prayer
and songbook for Israel. However, when you look
closely at this portion of Scripture, you will find that it's
more than a nice little song — it is truth from God's
Word!

## Put Yourself in Remembrance

From this psalm, we can see that David was stirring
himself up to praise the Lord. The tone indicates that he
had, perhaps, discovered a lack of thankfulness or grati
tude in his life.

Today we often lack thankfulness for what God has
done for us. We seem more concerned about needing
this, that, and the other thing than about thanking Him
for who He is and for what He has given us.

Now there's nothing wrong with praying for our
needs to be met and asking for God's blessings. If we're
sick, for example, we need healing; and, thank God, we
can ask Him for healing and receive it! But we've been

neglectful in thanking Him for the blessings we already have.

We sometimes need to be reminded that God is the giver of blessings and benefits, and we need to be thankful for that. Apparently, David needed to remind himself of all the Lord's benefits (Ps. 103:2), and we are no different.

## '. . . Who Forgives All Your Sins'

In verse 3, David begins to list specific benefits to be thankful for.

**PSALM 103:3**

**3  Who FORGIVES ALL YOUR SINS and heals all your diseases.**

Notice that the first thing David counted as a blessing was *the forgiveness of sin.* Think about that. If not for the mercy and grace of God, where would we be today? We all would be lost and on our way to hell. Many of us wouldn't even be alive. Some people know what it's like to be far out in sin and so addicted to drugs or alcohol that if not for the mercy of God, they wouldn't be alive today. They have experienced great deliverance because of God's forgiveness.

Many New Testament verses also tell us of God's mercy and His faithfulness to forgive sin. One of them is First John 1:9: *"If we confess our sins, he is faithful and just and will forgive us our sins and purify us from all unrighteousness"* (NIV).

If we are sorry for our sin and confess our sin to God, He is faithful not only to forgive us, but to purify us from all unrighteousness and restore us to a place of unbroken fellowship with Himself. Through Christ, we have received the remission of sin! And if we miss it after we've been born again, we can still receive the forgiveness and cleansing of sin!

## '. . . Who Heals All Your Diseases'

David named the forgiveness of sins as the first and foremost of God's benefits. Second, he named *healing.*

**PSALM 103:3**

**3  Who forgives all your sins AND HEALS ALL YOUR DISEASES.**

Notice from this verse that God forgives *all* of our sins and heals *all* of our diseases. "All" means *all!* "All" covers everything. That means it is applicable to all forms of sickness and disease. God doesn't just forgive *some* sins or heal *some* diseases. No, He has covered it all! God is able and willing to heal *all* sickness and disease!

Some people need healing of sicknesses that aren't very serious, naturally speaking. (That doesn't mean they aren't sick — because when you're sick, *you're sick!*) Others need healing of diseases that aren't terminal, but are incurable. Still others need healing of deadly diseases. They have received a bad report from doctors — in some cases, a "death sentence" because medical science holds no hope for them.

Thank God for His healing mercy! We need to be thankful for this blessing and benefit. We need to remember that this is the God we serve — One Who will forgive all of our sins and heal all of our diseases!

# '. . . Who Redeems Your Life From the Pit'

Third, David said, "Who redeems your life from the pit and crowns you with love and compassion" (Ps. 103:4 *NIV*). In the *King James Version*, this verse reads, *"Who redeemeth thy life from destruction. . . ."* Through Christ, God has redeemed us from *destruction*. He has rescued us from the dictatorship of the evil one. Through Jesus' death, burial, and resurrection, God has delivered us from the kingdom of tyranny's rule, and

has translated us into the Kingdom of His dear Son
(Col. 1:13)!

The devil is a cruel tyrant, an oppressor who rules
with an iron fist and tries to force or drive people to do
certain things. But God rules over us with a velvet glove
of love. He doesn't *force* us to do the right thing; we
*want* to do the right thing because, through the New
Birth, the love of God has been shed abroad in our
hearts by the Holy Ghost (Rom. 5:5).

As a parent, you can make your children do what's
right while they are living at home with you. But when
they reach adulthood and leave your house, you lose
the oversight and control that you had before. As adults,
they will do what they want to do. But isn't it rewarding
when they grow up and want to do right — when they
want to obey God and His Word from a heart of love
for you and God?

What else does it mean to be "redeemed from
destruction"? It means that God keeps us in the midst of
danger, sometimes when we're not even aware of it.
Psalm 91:11 says, *". . . he shall give his angels charge
over thee, to keep thee in all thy ways."* We need to
thank God for that!

There's so much we have to be thankful for that we
often don't even think about. But we can thank God for

the forgiveness of sin, for healing, and for redemption from destruction!

## '. . . Who Crowns You With Love and Compassion'

Fourth, David goes on to say in verse 4 that God *". . . crowns you with love and compassion" (NIV)*. In some dictionaries, the word crown means *to honor or reward*. And the Hebrew word for "crown" in this verse implies *to encircle or encompass for attack or protection*.

Hallelujah! God honors and rewards us when we set our love upon Him and thank and praise Him for His goodness and mercy. As we thank and praise Him privately, He will reward us openly. God crowns us with His love and compassion. Well, a crown can be seen, and it is *meant* to be seen. In the same way, God wants others to see what He is doing in our lives so *they* will want to know this God we are praising.

In the United States of America, the Stars and Stripes of our country's flag symbolize our unity and the price that was paid for our freedom. And that flag represents our continued freedom and the United States citizen's guaranteed right to enjoy certain benefits and privileges.

Similarly, because of two pieces of wood that formed the Cross on which our Savior hung on Golgatha's hill, we as Christians — as citizens of Heaven — are guaranteed freedom and certain Blood-bought benefits and privileges.

The Living Lamb of God laid down His life willingly. Soldiers pierced His hands and feet with nails, and thrust a spear into His side. He cried, "It is finished!" and gave up the ghost (John 19:30). Jesus paid the price to redeem our life — from sin, sickness, and destruction. He paid it all to give us all. He forgives all of our sins, and heals all of our diseases. He redeems our life from the pit of destruction. And He crowns us with His deep love and compassion

## God Invested in Us Richly So We Can Bless Others

God has invested in us His love and compassion. We are now to let that love and compassion become the distinguishing pattern of our lives as we await Jesus' return. We must share God's love and compassion with others, including the unsaved. We may not love the things they do, but we are commanded to love *them*. It's the goodness of God that leads people to repentance (Rom. 2:4), and the love of God that brings them into the Kingdom of God.

The Bible also says, *"My little children, let us not love in word, neither in tongue; but in deed and in truth"* (1 John 3:18). You see, it's not just words that show forth the love of God — it's words and deeds. It's heartfelt compassion. It's getting out and ministering to that person who's in trouble instead of having the attitude, "Well, if you had done the right thing to begin with, you wouldn't be in this mess." It's ministering to them on a positive note, rather than a negative one.

Where would we be if that had been God's attitude toward us before we were saved or when we've gotten ourselves into trouble *since* we were saved? No, God reached down to earth in the Person of Jesus Christ to extend a hand of love and to pull mankind up so that man could enter into glorious fellowship with Him.

## '. . . Who Satisfies Your Desires with Good Things'

Let's review the benefits we've looked at so far. First, we saw that God forgives all of our sins. Second, He heals all of our diseases (Ps. 103:3). Third, He redeems our life from the pit of destruction, and, fourth, He crowns us with love and compassion (v. 4).

Fifth, Psalm 103:5 says He, "satisfies your desires with good things so that your youth is renewed like the eagle's" (*NIV*).

Second Corinthians 4:16 says, "*. . . though our outward man perish* [or we could say, "gets older"], *yet the inward man is renewed day by day."* Although we will age in our bodies as long as we are on the earth, our spirits are alive unto God and can be renewed daily. We can remain youthful spiritually, and that can carry over into our physical bodies and even our minds.

For example, people are always asking me, "Rev. Hagin, how can you still run and play ball and enjoy sports the way you do?" Because my youth is being renewed like the eagle's!

Now I can't run quite as fast as I used to, but I can still run! I'm in pretty good physical shape. Mentally, I don't even think about getting older. I simply don't feel old for my age. My birth certificate indicates that I'm such-and-such years old, but I feel young — spiritually, mentally, and physically!

I have found the "fountain of youth" — it's right here in the Bible! God's Word is a fountain of youth, so drink from it daily. And when you think you're full, keep on drinking!

The following passage says more about God's promise to satisfy us with good things:

**JOEL 2:23-27**

**23 Be glad then, ye children of Zion, and rejoice in the Lord your God: for he hath given you the former rain moderately, and he will cause to come down for you the rain, the former rain, and the latter rain in the first month.**

**24 And the floors shall be full of wheat, and the fats shall overflow with wine and oil.**

**25 And I will restore to you the years that the locust hath eaten, the cankerworm, and the caterpiller, and the palmerworm, my great army which I sent among you.**

**26 And ye shall eat in plenty, and be satisfied, and praise the name of the Lord your God, that hath dealt wondrously with you: and my people shall never be ashamed.**

**27 And ye shall know that I am in the midst of Israel, and that I am the Lord your God,**

**and none else: and my people shall never be ashamed.**

In the *New International Version*, verse 23 says, ". . . he has given you the autumn rains in righteousness. He sends you abundant showers, both autumn and spring rains, as before."

Naturally speaking, farmers of certain kinds of crops know that they need rain at a certain time in early autumn and at a certain time in the spring if they are to have a good harvest. In other words, you need rain at the proper time. And in this passage, God promised this and other blessings to His people. In short, He promised them abundant living!

The following scriptures agree:

**JOHN 10:10**
**10 The thief cometh not, but for to steal, and to kill, and to destroy: I [Jesus] am come that they might have life, and that they might have it MORE ABUNDANTLY.**

**JOHN 10:10 (*NIV*)**
**10 The thief comes only to steal and kill and destroy; I have come that they may have life, and have it TO THE FULL.**

Jesus was talking about the people of God who would be under the New Covenant once His death, resurrection, and ascension were complete.

## Praise and Thanksgiving Will Stop the Enemy's Destruction

The thief — the devil — comes to steal, kill, and bring destruction to us, trying to destroy our harvest. It may be a harvest of healing or some other promised blessing. But Jesus said, "I came to bring life, and not just life, but life to the full!"

As you learn how to count your blessings and to live a lifestyle of praising God, you can stop the destruction of the enemy in its tracks. The devil is a defeated foe! Jesus defeated him through His death, burial, and resurrection. The power in thanksgiving and praise will cause you to step right *over* destruction and *into* life more abundantly — life to the full!

**PSALM 103:1**

**1  Bless the Lord, O MY SOUL: AND ALL THAT IS WITHIN ME, bless his holy name.**

David began and ended this verse by saying, "Bless the Lord" and "Bless His holy Name." Then right in the middle, he said, *". . . O my soul: and all that is within me. . . ."*

What was David saying? He was saying that from the depths of our being, from our inmost being, we should bless the Lord. In other words, from the bottom of our heart, we should continually be thanking and praising God for all He has done and is doing in our lives.

As we show forth joy and rejoicing from our heart, and count our many blessings, we will stay strong in our faith and positive in our attitude amidst a negative world full of despair. Our praise and thanksgiving will inspire others and open the door to even more, untold blessings in our own lives.

# Reasons To Rejoice

## six

*We've* looked at the powerful role praise and thanksgiving play in receiving from God and in experiencing manifestations of His goodness and power. But we still often have a more difficult time praising God during times of adversity than when everything is going smoothly in our lives. But is adversity a good reason to stop praising God?

To answer that question, look at what the prophet Habakkuk said about it:

**HABAKKUK 3:17,18 (*NIV*)**
**17 Though the fig-tree does not bud and there are no grapes on the vines, though the olive crop fails and the fields produce no food, though there are no sheep in the pen and no cattle in the stalls,**

**18 yet I will rejoice in the Lord, I will be joyful in God my Saviour.**

To give you a little background on this book of the Bible, it seems that the prophet Habakkuk was burdened that evil in the world was seemingly going unpunished. But God showed the prophet a divine plan in which the Chaldeans would be an instrument of judgment.

Then God showed the prophet that the Chaldean nation would later be destroyed, and God's glory would fill the earth. He encouraged Habakkuk that the plan would soon be fulfilled and that he should wait for it.

Sometimes God reveals something to us, yet it takes time for it to come to pass in our lives. And the thing that keeps people from success more than anything else is impatience. They are not willing to endure until God's will comes to pass in their lives. Impatience is always the forerunner of a negative lifestyle.

## Good Things Take Time

Most of us live in a society in which everybody wants what they want — and they want it "yesterday!" We live in a world of "fast everything." For example, rarely do we have the kind of biscuits at home anymore that are made from scratch (the way our parents and grandparents did it). Most of the time, we pop open a can, place pre-made biscuits in a baking pan, and bake them.

And we don't bake cakes and pies anymore. We buy them frozen or from a bakery. But, if you're like me, you much prefer the homemade kind! They taste better — but they take more time.

Thank God for the modern conveniences of life. However, things that are more valuable or worthwhile often take more time to produce. This principle holds true in many areas. For example, my dad used to tell me when I was a kid, "Son, if something is worth doing, it's worth doing right, or don't do it at all."

Some things just simply can't be rushed if they are to reach their fullest potential. Sometimes walking by faith requires us to wait. So spend your waiting time in praise!

In a previous chapter, I mentioned that the Bible tells us repeatedly that we are to live by our faith. The prophet Habakkuk said it in Habakkuk 2:4: ". . . *the just shall live by his faith.*"

We've also seen that praise is an expression of our faith. Habakkuk confirms this truth. After the prophet said that the just would live by his faith, he vowed, as recorded in Habakkuk 3:17,18, to rejoice in the Lord no matter what adversity befell him. Why would he rejoice in the midst of such problems and trouble? Because he was living by his faith!

We can live by faith and praise God even in the midst of the storm. In times of greatest difficulty, we can rejoice in the Lord and expect great victory.

## Rejoice in Adversity

You might say, "Yes, but you're talking about a prophet. Certainly, Habakkuk could rejoice when everything was going wrong."

But Habakkuk didn't rejoice because he was a prophet. He didn't rejoice because of his anointing or calling. He rejoiced only because of what he knew about God through God's unchangeable Word. And that's why we, too, can rejoice today. When circumstances change for the worse, we can rejoice in the Lord because we know that His Word has *not* changed!

You can and should rejoice in adversity. No matter what storm of life you find yourself in, you can rejoice in the Lord. Your circumstances may have changed from good to bad — or from bad to worse! It may look as though you're doing down in defeat. But God's Word has not changed, and His unchanging Word has enough power in it to turn your situation around and raise you up victorious!

Let's look again at Habakkuk 3:17,18. In verse 17, he said, *"Though the fig-tree does not bud . . ." (NIV).*

If a fruit tree doesn't bud or blossom, that means it's not going to produce a harvest of fruit that season.

Habakkuk went on to say, ". . . and there are no grapes on the vines, though the olive crop fails and the fields produce no food . . . ."

What was the prophet saying? He was saying that people were going to be hungry because there wasn't going to be any food to be picked or harvested.

Then he added, ". . . though there are no sheep in the pen and no cattle in the stalls." That meant they would have no livestock to kill and eat either.

What a bleak picture! This scenario indicated that they were going to starve! God had shown the prophet the difficult times that lay ahead. So what was Habakkuk's attitude about it? He said, "I'm going to rejoice in God, anyway!"

## Rejoice *Anyway!*

Even when political and economical markers seem to predict difficult times ahead, we shouldn't wring our hands in worry and fear, wondering what will happen next. It's important to remember that in the midst of any change or upheaval, God and His Word will not change! So rejoice in the Lord!

The following scriptures assure us that God has never changed — and He never will!

**MALACHI 3:6**
**6 . . . I am the Lord, I change not.**

**HEBREWS 13:8**
**8 Jesus Christ the same yesterday, and to day, and for ever.**

So rejoice! God is still on the throne. Jesus is still King of kings and Lord of lords! God is still the Almighty One, your Deliverer, your Provider, the great I AM. *Your circumstances can't change God, but God can change your circumstances!*

As a believer, your trust is not in the economic system or even in your job. Your trust is in God and His everlasting Word. (*See* Matt. 24:35; Mark 13:31; and Luke 21:33.)

**1 PETER 1:24,25**
**24 For all flesh *is* as grass, and all the glory of man as the flower of grass. The grass withereth, and the flower thereof falleth away:**

## 25 But the word of the Lord endureth for ever.

You *are* who God's Word says you are. You *have* what God's Word says you have. And you *can do* what God's Word says you can do. If God's Word says you've been delivered — *and it does* — then you are delivered! And that fact cannot be changed, as far as you're concerned, if you will hold on to that truth and never let go.

The devil will try to tell you that you're going under in defeat. He will try to convince you to throw in the towel and quit. But you need to get hold of the reality of God's Word and refuse to let it go. You need to be fully persuaded that what God promised, He is able also to perform (Rom. 4:21). You need to have the attitude, "I cannot be defeated, and I will not quit!"

Someone asked, "Why do you always say, 'I cannot be defeated, and I will not quit'?" I have always lived by that saying because it's based on the Word of God. The Word of God tells me that I cannot be defeated if I will not quit.

You might ask, "Well, isn't that a rather simplistic attitude?"

Maybe. But it has seen me through many problems, tests, and trials. The simplicity and the utter faithfulness of God's Word have gotten me this far, and will take me on until the Day of Jesus Christ — until Christ returns for His Church.

## Confident in the Savior

The prophet proclaimed in Habakkuk 3:18, *"Yet I will rejoice in the Lord, I will be joyful in God my Savior"* (*NIV*). No matter what the problem or circumstance, you can also *be confident in the Savior.*

Jesus has overcome the world. He has overcome Satan and sin. He defeated Satan in awful combat, emerged victorious in His resurrection, and now sits in Heaven with the Father. So no matter what problem or circumstance arises, you can be confident in the Savior. When trouble comes near, you can be confident that you have a Friend who's nearer. He is the Friend who sticks closer than a brother (Prov. 18:24)!

When tests and trials come, too many Christians sit down with their crying towel and have the attitude, "Woe is me! Lord, why did You let this happen to me?"

It is a sad fact, but true, nevertheless. Instead of crying, they should be rejoicing. They should rise to their feet and proclaim, "This is the day that the Lord has made. I will rejoice and be glad in it!" (Ps. 118:24).

There's not enough trouble in this world or enough devils in hell to keep you from rejoicing in Jesus your Savior or from receiving what belongs to you according to God's Word! So let us rejoice in the Savior. Let us rejoice in the life of victory that is ours. Our life-source is not of this world — it's out of this world! It's heavenly!

## A Supernatural Glide

Habakkuk 3:19 says, *"The Sovereign Lord is my strength; he makes my feet like the feet of a deer, he enables me to go on the heights. . ."* (*NIV*). Have you ever watched a deer in the wild? A deer's feet are quick and sure! To see deer racing effortlessly across a field or meadow is a beautiful sight. When an obstacle gets in their way, they go right over the top of it. They leap high and glide through the air, landing gracefully on the other side.

Remember, Jesus said that we are *in* the world, but not *of* the world. So don't let troubles get you down! Just go right over the top of them as you rejoice in God, the source of your strength!

In the midst of trouble, God can make your feet like that of a deer. In other words, by faith, you won't be hemmed in by the circumstances. You can leap *over* circumstances. And you won't be running in your own strength. *God* will enable you to run the race that is set before you. And as you yield to Him and His strength, He will cause you to step into blessings that you've never even imagined.

However, you won't walk in those blessings if you allow yourself to remain hemmed in by the tests, trials, and circumstances that befall you. In other words, if you wring your hands in worry, doubt, and unbelief, your feet will not be made like those of the deer, able to go on the heights (Hab. 3:19 *NIV*).

But as you rejoice in the Savior and His unchanging Word and take hold of His strength, you will hurdle over the circumstances and land right in the middle of the blessings of God!

Someone might say, "Rev. Hagin, I don't *want* to be hemmed in by circumstances. But the circumstances are real. What am I supposed to do?"

*Rejoice in the Lord!* In spite of the hard times, *rejoice!* When the storms of life blow, rejoice in the Word, in the Savior, and in God's sure strength. God will lift you up to a higher place if you will rejoice in Him!

# Faith's 'Costume'

When you're faced with troubles, you can take hold of God's strength. You can go into the "phone booth" and come out with your cape and costume and the word "Faith" written across your chest! You can become undefeatable to the enemy, because your strength is not your own; your strength is of God.

That's a simple analogy based on a fictional cartoon character, but we can learn something from it. When problems challenge us, we need to get out of our "regular" clothes — we need to get out of trying to do things in our own strength. Instead, we need to clothe ourselves with the garment of faith and the strength of God.

You see, when you try to overcome tests and trials in your own strength, the devil can defeat you. But in God, you can't go under. He is your strength!

**ACTS 17:28**

**28 . . . in him [God] we live, and move, and have our being.**

Someone asked, "I wonder what's going to happen with our economy?" I don't know, but I do know that in Him I live and move and have my being!

Just as God took care of the children of Israel by delivering them from Egypt, by leading them safely across the Red Sea, and by sustaining them as they wandered across the desert, He can take care of you and me!

Just as He took care of His people when they finally crossed the Jordan River and began to subdue the land that belonged to them, He can surely take care of us as we subdue the land that belongs to us!

We can talk about how bad things are, or we can talk about how good God is and how good things are with God. Trials may come and go, but during the good times and the bad, the Lord is our strength. We don't have to have the solution to the problem. We don't have to fix the problem in our own strength. We don't have to be strong enough to take care of the situation. The Lord is our problem solver.

## Your Strength Can Be Renewed

Many Christians today are living a life of overwhelming fear. But they shouldn't be, based on this verse:

**PSALM 27:1**
**1   The Lord is my light and my salvation; whom shall I fear? The Lord is the strength of my life; of whom shall I be afraid?**

That verse should cause us to rejoice and shout! The Lord is our light and our salvation. Leaning on the everlasting arms of God, we don't have any justification for being afraid. He is our strength, and we can take on His strength and be strong in Him.

As we rejoice in God as the source of our strength, He will renew our strength, and give us a spring in our step so that we can keep right on marching down the highway of victory.

### ISAIAH 40:31

**31 But those who hope in the Lord will renew their strength.**

If you have a cordless electric shaver, you know that you can charge it and use it at full power for a while. But after a period of time, the charge starts to weaken, and you have to recharge the shaver's battery before the shaver will operate at full power again.

Similarly, we need to renew our strength in the Lord. We can't keep operating at full power without staying vitally connected to Him. We must stay "plugged in," or we will lose power.

If you feel your strength beginning to wane, just start rejoicing in the Lord and in His strength. He will "recharge" you.

Replenish your spiritual strength by reading His Word and waiting before Him as you praise Him and sing psalms, hymns, and spiritual songs (Eph. 5:19). You can also renew your strength by praying in the Spirit, building yourself up in your most holy faith (Jude 20).

# Soar Like the Eagle

### ISAIAH 40:31 (*NIV*)
**31 . . . They** [who hope in the Lord] **will soar on wings like eagles.**

Have you ever seen an eagle soar? Eagles don't bother much with things below, even things that are a hundred feet above the ground. No, they can soar much higher than that! They spread their wings to catch a current of wind and they allow that current to cause them to glide high into the atmosphere.

Eagles don't expend much energy as they soar to those great heights. With outstretched wings, they use the wind to carry them. Then looking downward with their piercing eyes, eagles spot a morsel of food, and they use their energy for diving for prey. Then they use their strength again for their ascent until they catch another current of wind that will take them to the high places.

Friend, you may feel "knocked down" by the enemy. You may have been soaring along like an eagle when you were dealt a blow of circumstances that caught you off guard and sent you plummeting to the ground. Rejoice! God is the source of your strength. In Him, you have what it takes to reach those high places again!

**ISAIAH 40:31 (*NIV*)**
**31 . . . they** [who hope in the Lord] **will run and not grow weary, they will walk and not be faint.**

Why does the Lord want us to run and not grow weary, and to walk and not faint? So we won't faint and give up in our faith. God wants to turn around those circumstances that have tried to defeat us!

Our problems can no longer hold us down! They can't hold us back! They can't keep us from walking in the victory that is ours!

Right in the midst of trouble, I exhort you to:

Rejoice! God hasn't changed!

Rejoice! God has given you a Savior!

Rejoice! God has given you strength!

Rejoice, Rejoice, Rejoice, Rejoice!

Rejoice, and again I say, Rejoice!

# God Wants You To Change Your Mind!

*Finally*, *brethren, whatsoever things are true, whatsoever things are honest,whatsoever things are just, whatsoever things are pure, whatsoever things are lovely, whatsoever things are of good report; if there be any virtue, and if there be any praise, THINK ON THESE THINGS.*

— Philippians 4:8

*For my thoughts are not your thoughts, neither are your ways my ways, saith the Lord. For as the heavens are higher than the earth, so are my ways higher than your ways, and my thoughts than your thoughts.*

— Isaiah 55:8,9

How many times have you heard someone say, "That can't be done," when someone had a dream or idea of doing something big? I know pastors who have presented building programs or other projects to their church only to see their plan grind to a halt by this wrong attitude of negativism and defeat.

If we're not careful, a worldly attitude can get into the church, and that attitude will stop faith in its tracks. How can we avoid this snare? By prayer and by reprogramming our thinking in line with God's Word.

The world programs us to think negatively, but Romans 12:2 says, *". . . be not conformed to this world: but be ye transformed by the renewing of your mind, that ye may prove what is that good, and acceptable, and perfect, will of God."*

We can be transformed — *changed* — from having a negative attitude to having a positive attitude by spending time in the Word of God. We can train ourselves to think in line with God, not with the world.

If you're familiar with computers, you know that someone has to program a computer before it will function. And if a computer ever "crashes," it will probably have to be reprogrammed.

A computer will only do what it is programmed to do. Well, in a sense, our mind is the greatest computer ever made. God put it together with memory banks in which to hold or store certain information. And your "computer" will only do what it has been programmed to do.

For example, if you grew up in a home where your parents were negative and critical, then you have probably dealt with being negative and critical yourself. But the good news is, you can take the Word of God and reprogram your mind. And as the Word instills a positive mental outlook, it will also override a negative one. You can use the Word of God to "delete" your old way of thinking and replace it with a new way of thinking to help you press on to victory.

So what new thoughts do we think? Paul tells us in Philippians 4.

**PHILIPPIANS 4:8 (*NIV*)**
**8 Finally, brothers, whatever is true, whatever is noble, whatever is right, whatever is pure, whatever is lovely, whatever is admirable — if anything is excellent or praiseworthy — think about such things.**

Now that's *not* the way the world thinks. For instance, most of the things reported by the news media do not fit the criteria laid out in this verse. Although the news reports of events may be true, they are often not pure, lovely, admirable, or praiseworthy.

Thank God, some of the things reported by the media are admirable and praiseworthy. But by far, most of the things we hear and see are negative. If we're not careful, we can start to think about those things more than about the Word of God.

We know that wrong thinking produces wrong believing. And wrong believing produces wrong actions, and wrong actions will produce wrong results. But right thinking, believing, and acting in line with God's Word will help us develop a positive outlook and produce whatever we need from God's Word!

## Reprogram: Talk and Act Differently

Did you ever notice that God blesses people who come to Him with thanksgiving and an attitude of confidence? For instance, take Caleb's attitude: "Give me this mountain — not because of who I am, but because of who God is" (Joshua 14:12)!

God blesses people who take hold of His Word and refuse to let go. God blesses those who are confident in Him and His Word and who are positive in spite of negative circumstances.

You can't take hold of the Word and let it dominate your thoughts and actions without becoming a positive person. Likewise, you can't be a person of the Word

and be negative — unless you allow your natural mind
to take over.

## A Renewed Mind Is Positive and Steadfast

Your natural mind is governed by your senses —
what you can see, hear, taste, touch, and smell. And the
natural mind will always lean toward being ruled by circumstances, whether good or bad. But the mind
renewed with the Word of God remains positive and
steadfast no matter how dark the circumstances.

The Holy Spirit is a gentleman. But the devil is *not!*
The Holy Ghost will nudge you and lead you in line
with God's Word, and will bring scriptures to your
remembrance that you have read or heard. But the devil
will throw wrong thoughts at you and try to attack your
mind with thoughts that are contrary to God's Word. If
you don't stand against those thoughts and chase them
away with the Word of God, the devil will take over! He
will try to take over your mind and your life.

Second Corinthians 10:5 says, *"CASTING DOWN
IMAGINATIONS, and every high thing that exalteth itself
against the knowledge of God, and bringing into captivity
every thought to the obedience of Christ."*

We must keep watch over what goes into our minds.
This can certainly be a challenge in our day of "instant

communication." The technology of this generation is a mixed blessing. For example, we can know what happened on the other side of the world within minutes of its happening. That can have a negative effect because through this instant communication, we are bombarded with the live coverage of the aftermath of school shootings, police chases and standoffs, and even war!

We didn't have the communications technology during World War II that we have today. In those days, by the time the American public heard any news about a particular battle, two or three weeks had passed. However, during the two Gulf Wars, we received minute-by-minute coverage, saw footage of planes flying over targets, and watched real bombs explode right before our eyes!

## The Words You Hear Will Affect Your Outlook

Psychological dangers are associated with receiving constant negative communication. Medical science holds convincing evidence that people who are negative, or who live in a negative environment, have more physical ailments and recover less quickly than those with a positive outlook.

Well, we who know the Bible have known this all along! The Bible says, *"A cheerful heart is good medicine, but a crushed spirit dries up the bones"* (Prov. 17:22 *NIV*). You see, you can't have a cheerful heart and be negative at the same time.

We need to do all we can to receive faith-building words into our lives, not negative, destructive words. We can do that by maintaining a consistent devotional life, and beginning every day with thanksgiving to God. We need to fellowship with him continually and make time daily for reading His Word.

The devil and this world will constantly bombard our mind to try to pull our attention away from the Word and onto negativism — fear, doubt, and unbelief. The devil knows that if he can get our attention off the Word and focused on negative thoughts instead, he can defeat us.

Some Christians read the Word one time and think they are renewing their mind. But, no, it is a continual process, and we must do it if we want to break the power of negativity in our lives.

## How To Change Your Mind for the Better

Well, exactly how are we going to change our mind — our attitude and our thinking? Romans 12:2 says, *"And be not conformed to this world: but be ye transformed by the renewing of your mind" (NIV).*

God wants us to be transformed, *changed*, by the renewing of our mind. He wants us to become established in His Word to the point that when a problem arises, His Word is the first thing that comes out our mouth. In other words, we respond to the tests and trials of life with the Word, not with our own natural reasoning.

Remember that right thinking produces right believing, and right believing produces right acting. Many people are only *mentally agreeing* with the Bible, but God wants us to *believe* it! He wants us to believe it so much that we'll act on it. Only then will we see the results that we desire.

## Thoughts Produce Beliefs; Beliefs Produce Actions

When someone believes something, he acts like it's so. For instance, let's say you live near a pond, and in the dead of winter, the pond freezes over. You say to a friend, "I believe that ice is thick enough to walk on."

Your friend responds, "Yes, I agree."

Then you say, "Well, since you agree, just go ahead and step out on the ice."

Your friend answers, "Well, uh, I believe the ice is thick enough, all right, but I'm not going to step out on it."

Your friend doesn't really believe that ice will hold him up.

You see, many people will quickly agree with God's Word, but when it comes to actually putting His Word to the test, not nearly as many will do that! They won't go that far, because they're not committed to the integrity of God's holy Word.

When you believe God's Word from your heart, you will act like it's so. You will be positive in your attitude. You will rejoice with praise and thanksgiving. Why? Because you know that your God is El-Shaddai, the God Who's More Than Enough and Who helps you press beyond your limits in time of trouble!

# Pressing Beyond the Limits

## eight

*Within* man lies the desire to press beyond certain natural limitations. For example, we have pressed beyond prior limits in flight and in space travel. *Flash Gordon* and some of the older television shows about space are no longer fantasy. We have gone beyond the earth's gravitational pull, beyond the sound barrier, and so forth. (And we haven't seen the end yet!)

We have also reached beyond the limits in technology and communications — from the telephone to wireless communication to the Internet, and even to satellite communication. We have gone far beyond the limits of the past.

Medical research has also surpassed many limitations of the past. For example, I read a magazine article about the development of a computer-type chip that

93

can be implanted into the eyes of certain blind patients to give them sight!

It seems we are constantly being challenged with new opportunities to believe God beyond what we've believed Him for in the past, in both natural and spiritual matters.

In this chapter, I want to look into pressing beyond natural limitations from the spiritual perspective.

# One Man Who Pressed Beyond the Limits

Let's look at the life of Abraham, a man who was exceedingly blessed and became known as the "Father of Faith" because he pressed beyond the limits.

> **ROMANS 4:19-21**
> **19 And being not weak in faith, he consid-ered not his own body now dead, when he was about an hundred years old, neither yet the deadness of Sara's womb:**
> **20 He staggered not at the promise of God through unbelief; but was strong in faith, giving glory to God;**
> **21 And being fully persuaded that, what he had promised, he was able also to perform.**

At one hundred years of age, Abraham did not con-sider the limitations of his body. He only looked at what God had said — that he and Sarah would have a child!.

The limitations of the body said, "It is not possible."

But God said, "It *is* possible!"

Verse 19 says, ". . . [Abraham] *being not weak in faith, he considered not . . . .*" Abraham believed the promise of God and pressed beyond natural limitations. He reached beyond his physical limitations because he had a strong faith in God.

## Excuses Will Keep You Bound by Limits

Many people make excuses for not taking opportunities God lays before them. They consider their limitations and say to God, "I'm too young," "I'm too old," or "I'm too *this* or *that*," or "I'm not smart enough" or "I'm not educated enough."

But what does God's Word say? If Abraham had considered his limitations, he would have said to God, "No way, God. It's not possible. I'm too old. It will never happen." And it wouldn't have happened!

But we know that Abraham received the promise, and became the father of many nations, just as God had promised. He did not consider his own limitations; He considered his limitless God!

And even after Abraham received his promised son, Isaac, Abraham went beyond the limits again when, in obedience to God, he took the boy and headed up a mountain to sacrifice his son. Abraham went so far as to build an altar and put the boy — the one who was born beyond natural limitations — on the altar.

Abraham did all this in complete obedience, because he knew his God, and he refused to back off his faith. And just in time, God showed Abraham a ram caught in some bushes, and Abraham sacrificed the ram instead of the boy.

**GENESIS 22:12,13**

**12 And he** [the Angel of the Lord] **said, Lay not thine hand upon the lad, neither do thou any thing unto him: for now I know that thou fearest God, seeing thou hast not withheld thy son, thine only son from me.**
**13 And Abraham lifted up his eyes, and looked, and behold behind him a ram caught in a thicket by his horns: and Abraham went and took the ram, and offered him up for a burnt offering in the stead of his son.**

This was a test of Abraham's faith — to prove he was someone who really believed God would provide.

And God provided! He provided a sacrifice for Abraham, and established His covenant with the "Father of Faith," a covenant of which Christians became beneficiaries through Christ (Gen. 22:1-14).

*God has no limits.* And He is the same today as He was in Abraham's day. The only limitations God has as far as we are concerned are the limits we place on Him through our doubt and unbelief.

*If you can believe, you can receive!*

Abraham believed God and pressed beyond his limitations, and many nations were born from the fulfill ment of that one promise. Today, God is trying to get you to look beyond your limitations and to look at His promises. If He promised it, you can have it.

So many Christians need to rise to their full stature, spiritually. They need to walk in God's strength and have a backbone of steel instead of a "backbone of string." Then they can stand in the face of every obstacle and every challenge to their faith and shout, "God said it, I believe it, and that settles it! You say it can't happen, but God says it will!"

Limitations will say, "You can't." And if you focus on the limitations, you *can't*. But God says, "You can!" If you focus on Him, you will find that you *can!*

## Jesus Demonstrated God's Limitless Power

In His earth walk, Jesus demonstrated the limitless power of God. He spent three years with a select group of men, His disciples, who were for the most part uneducated men. In other words, they were not considered to be in society's elite class. But He walked with them as their leader and teacher for three years, demonstrating the power of God. He healed the sick, cured the blind and the deaf, delivered demon-oppressed and demon-possessed individuals, and raised the dead. Then He told His followers, *"I tell you the truth, anyone who has faith in me will do what I have been doing. He will do even greater things than these, because I am going to the Father"* (John 14:12 *NIV*).

When Jesus was crucified on the Cross, before He died, He looked up to the sky and said, "It is finished!" Then His head slumped to His chest, and He gave up the ghost (John 19:30). At that, Jesus' disciples, looking to their own limitations and the seeming hopelessness of the situation, scattered. They hid themselves. They weren't thinking about Jesus' promise; they were thinking only about how powerless, helpless, and afraid they felt without Him.

# The Power Behind the Promise

But one great day as they were all sitting together in one place in Jerusalem, a rushing mighty wind blew through that place! They heard a sound from Heaven as of a mighty wind, they saw "cloven tongues as of fire" which sat upon each of them, and they were filled with the Holy Ghost and began to speak in other tongues (Acts 2:1-4)!

Had it not been for what happened on the Day of Pentecost, Jesus' followers couldn't have carried out the promise Jesus made to them of doing the "greater works." They couldn't have gone beyond their own limitations.

We, too, need this power of Pentecost to do the works of Jesus, and the greater works He spoke of, in our generation. We need the Word of God and the Spirit of God to help us take the limits off and step over to receive our promised blessings. With the devil, circumstances, and the voice of the flesh screaming at us, "You won't make it!", we can fearlessly proclaim, "We are able! God is on our side! He is limitless in power, and He will see us through!"

The baptism in the Holy Spirit is all about power for the Age in which we live. It's about power beyond the natural world that takes us beyond our limitations into the realm of our limitless God!

## God Can Turn Your 'Little' Into Much

If you don't limit God and just believe Him, He will take what little you have and give you what you don't have! He will multiply your "little" and abundantly meet your need. For example, in First Kings 17, the widow said to Elijah, "I have a little meal and a little oil to make one last cake for my son and me so that we can eat it and die" (v. 12).

In other words, she said, "I have limitations." Her focus was on what little provision she had left. But the man of God said something that sounded strange. "Make me something to eat first" (v. 13). I'm sure his request overwhelmed her. All she could see was her lack — her limitations — and the prophet wanted her to give away what little she had left! But when she chose to go with God and put her focus on Him, she went beyond her limitations! God multiplied her "little," and she had plenty of meal and oil to feed herself, her son, and the prophet during a time of famine (vv. 14-16).

In the face of so many new things that threaten our existence today, our efforts to overcome them would be considered "little." But if we place our faith in God, He will multiply what "little" we have — by adding His supernatural power.

## Excuses Will Keep You Bound by Limits — Obedience Will Set You Free!

We need to stop limiting God in our life and go ahead and obey Him and His Word. When we yield to Him and His power, we will find that God will cause us to go beyond our own limitations — and even beyond the limitations others have placed on us.

For instance, when finances get tight, we should thank God for our jobs. And certainly, we should show respect and appreciation to those who pay our salaries. But if we allow our job to be our source, we limit God and His provision for us.

God can provide for you beyond your job, so don't look at your job as your sole support and source of income. Don't limit God; *He* is your source.

Some people have learned not to limit God in one or more areas of their lives — in the area of finances, for example — but they still limit Him in other areas. We need to remove *all* limits from God where our lives are concerned.

It's God's hour to move as He has never moved in our midst before. God wants to demonstrate His power in greater and greater ways to our generation. But it's going to take people who are willing to step out beyond human limitations and yield to the Spirit of God — people who are not afraid to step out with nothing under them but the Word of God!

## Manifestations of the Spectacular

In Second Kings 6, we read the account of the sons of the prophets who were building a new, larger home where they could dwell. One man had borrowed an ax, and as he was cutting down a tree, the ax head came off and fell into the water near Jordan. The man said to the prophet Elisha, *". . . Alas, master! for it was borrowed"* (2 Kings 6:5).

Elisha cut off a stick from a bush or tree and cast it into the water where the ax head had sunk. And, immediately, the iron ax head floated to the top of the water (v. 6)!

Friend, that's beyond the limitation of the natural, because iron doesn't float! Yet that time, it did!

God is the same today as He was when Elisha and all the great patriarchs of old were on the earth. We need to take the limits off our expectations. Today's

economic and political climate affords a perfect oppor-
tunity for God to show up in spectacular ways. And
He's not at a loss for meeting the needs of His people.
Nothing the world can throw at you is too big for Him.
He always has a way to balance things in your favor. If
He needs "to make an ax head float" for you, He will
do it! If . . . you will only believe.

There is a saying in the world, "The sky is the limit."

No! The sky is not the limit. *Heaven* is the limit! It's
not a question of what God can do; it's a question of
what we can believe.

In the natural, we live under the limitation of science —
of certain scientific laws. But a floating ax head illustrates
that the power of God defies laws of science. It's as if the
man of God, Elisha, were saying, "Let me show you the
powers of the Age to come. It's the same power that set
the worlds into existence" (Heb. 6:5, 11:3).

## 'Lose Your Mind' and Become a Success!

You might say, "Well, I don't want to limit God. I
want to be a person of the Word and learn the ways of
the Spirit. But I'm afraid people will think I'm crazy if I
go all out for God."

God wants us to change our way of thinking from
the world's way to His way.

That's what I mean when I say, "'Lose your mind' and become a success!"

Don't ever worry about what people think of you — about whether they will think you're crazy if you go all out for God. In today's environment, taking a stand for God could be a matter of life and death. So why worry what they think about your not limiting God in your life?

Proverbs 3:5 says, *"Trust in the Lord with all thine heart; and lean not unto thine own understanding."* In other words, trust in the Lord with all your heart, and do not lean to your own mind or your own natural, human way of thinking.

## God Wants To Demonstrate His Power

We need to break through our limitations and show the world our limitless God. When we do, and when others witness and experience for themselves manifestations of His glory, they will recognize the power of God. They will have to acknowledge that there is no way that man with his natural limitations could have accomplished such wonders on his own.

God can take us beyond our limits and He will receive glory for it in the presence of unbelievers. He was glorified on many such occasions in the life of the Apostle Paul. For example, when Paul was shipwrecked

on the island of Melita as a prisoner, as he was putting
some firewood on a fire, a viper came *". . . out from the
heat, and fastened on his hand"* (Acts 28:3). Now here
Paul had an opportunity to not limit God and to experience His delivering power!

**ACTS 28:4-6 (*NIV*)**
**4   When the islanders saw the snake hang-
ing from his** [Paul's] **hand, they said to each
other, "This man must be a murderer; for
though he escaped from the sea, Justice has
not allowed him to live."**
**5   But Paul shook the snake off into the fire
and suffered no ill effects.**
**6   The people expected him to swell up or
suddenly fall dead, but after waiting a long
time and seeing nothing unusual happen to
him, they changed their minds. . . .**

The people of the island knew that the snake was
venomous. At first, they thought Paul was a murderer
and that justice was going to be served by his being
killed by the snake. They thought he would die, but
Paul just shook the viper off into the fire and went on
about his business! He suffered no ill effect because God
helped him go beyond the limitations of the natural!

Now I'm not saying that we should handle snakes — that would be tempting God, and that would be foolish. And, certainly, if you were bitten by a snake, you should exercise natural precautions and seek out an antidote or professional help if possible — at the same time, believing God for your healing.

While I'm on the subject, I wouldn't let my confidence in a doctor or hospital get in the way of my believing God. My faith in Him would be first, before their recommendations. Doctors are human, too, and they have limitations. They do good work, but God is a limitless God; He can give wisdom to doctors beyond their natural knowledge. God can speed up the healing process, and He can deliver and save when doctors have done all they can do!

Paul didn't consider the limitations involved with being bitten by a highly poisonous viper; instead, he considered his limitless God. He was shipwrecked on an island of what the Bible calls "barbarians" (Acts 28:4). Apparently, Paul had no choice but to believe God beyond his own limitations. Paul *knew* the God he believed in, and he *knew* that He was willing and able to deliver him. And God delivered him!

## Your Victory in God Lies Beyond Your Own Limitations

If the devil can get you to consider your limitations —
whether it's limitations of your body, your mind, or your
finances — he will defeat you. But if God can get you to
take one step beyond your own limits, He will give you
victory!

That's where faith is — one step beyond our own
limits. And that's where God's victory is — beyond our
limits. When we understand what a limitless God we
serve, and that He is good and He loves us, we will tap
into His power that has no limit. We will soar to new
heights of victory and success that we never thought
possible!

The power of God is here, and it is available to us.
There are no limits to what we can receive from God.
Whatever it is you need, God has it. And it belongs to
you in Christ. You can receive it right now by faith!

Power companies use transformers to limit or regu-
late the flow of electrical power. Spiritually speaking, the
devil wants to put a transformer in your life to limit the
power of God that you receive. But God wants you to
take off the transformer so that more of His limitless
power can flow! To do that, you need to know and

believe what God's Word says, and you need to continually say what God's Word says. Only then will you take
hold of God's resources to press beyond your limits.

# The Triumph of Faith —
# Life Beyond Limitations

## nine

*"How long will the wicked, O Lord, how long will the wicked be jubilant?"*

— Psalm 94:3 (*NIV*)

The Psalmist David asked this question of the Lord, and, perhaps, you, too, have uttered the same words or at least held the same question in your mind.

This question seems relevant for our day. We see wickedness all around us, and sometimes it appears as if the wicked are prevailing. Around the world, threats of terrorism are ongoing. We've already experienced two Gulf Wars with constant rumors of more wars. We hear about crime wave after crime wave as gangs fight each other for more territory, and corporations resort to fraud to gain ground against their competitors. Many who are hungry for more money and power have a

109

"dog-eat-dog" mentality as they reach for the top, and they don't care whom they hurt along the way.

Everywhere we look, we can see many good people struggling to triumph over obstacles and enemies. And, often, justice seems to be nowhere in sight. It's enough to cause a negative attitude — if we allow it.

## The Battle of Survival

But God is a God of justice, and He doesn't want His people caught up in a battle of survival, attempting in their own strength to triumph over the opposition that challenges them. Our limitless God doesn't want His children struggling with limitations that have been placed before them. God doesn't want us to just *survive* — He wants us to *thrive!* He wants us to live beyond limitations.

God designed man to triumph over the limitations of life. God put something inside man that causes him or her to want to win over adversity. It seems that some are more motivated than others, but almost everyone has within him or her the desire to achieve and excel in life.

## Against All Odds

We are fascinated by people who have defied the odds and won battles that were by all appearances "un-winnable." We have tremendous respect for those who come from obscurity to prominence because of their indomitable spirit and their will to succeed. We are motivated and inspired by their stories of victory over hardship and by their zeal for life and for winning. We are attracted to their positive attitude.

Kurt Warner is the quarterback for the St. Louis Rams, the NFL team that won the Super Bowl in January of 2000. Did you know that just a few years before he became a Super Bowl quarterback, he was a stocker at a grocery store?

Another young man, Bill Bates, went from the University of Tennessee to the Dallas Cowboys to play football. Critics said he was too small and too slow, and that he'd never make it big. But for more than ten years, against all odds, no one could beat him out of his position on the team.

Have you ever been told to throw in the towel and quit? Have you ever been told you weren't going to make it? If you have, something inside you resisted that idea, because God put within you the desire to win!

Some years ago at the Winter Olympics, millions of Americans sat "glued" to their television sets as the American hockey team squared off against the Russian team for the gold medal. Experts and analysts predicted an overwhelming victory for the mighty Russian team. But when the final buzzer sounded, the Americans had defeated the Russian team, and American fans roared in unspeakable joy!

Although I was at home alone at the time, I jumped and hollered all over my living room — along with millions of others as they watched in their homes! Afterward, it seemed you couldn't go anywhere without hearing people talk about the remarkable feat accomplished by those young American men. They weren't supposed to have won the gold medal, but they did — against all odds! They had a winning spirit about them. Something inside of them said, "We are winners!"

It seems that we are constantly striving to be the best we can be and to exceed previous successes and achievements, whether they be our own or those of others. For example, although several people have climbed Mount Everest over the years, most of us remember only the first man to do it, Sir Edmund Hillary.

## Winning Counts — Big Time!

Mankind is fascinated by those who have reached notable heights of success and achievement against all probabilities of doing so. One of our nation's great presidents, Abraham Lincoln, experienced failure time and time again in his political quests. But he never gave up, and he eventually became one of the most revered presidents to grace the Oval Office. His approach to life was, "I cannot be defeated, and I will not quit!" It's a theme I have carried with me over the years.

Many people start businesses on a shoestring, and from those humble beginnings, they build great family fortunes. Some people start small, but they have a big dream, and they realize those dreams *beyond* what they envisioned. For example, a man from Bentonville, Arkansas, started one such enterprise. His name was Sam Walton. His work began in 1962 with a single Wal-Mart, which eventually developed into a chain of thousands of discount stores. Today, Wal-Mart is the world's number one retailer.

These feats and achievements I've mentioned are things people have accomplished with their own natural drive — because God instilled within them the desire to win.

When it comes to participating in sports, I am very competitive. I like to win.

Some will argue that it's not whether you win or lose, but how you play the game that counts. Certainly, I agree that good sportsmanship should be the rule, regardless of whether you win or lose. And I also agree that if a person plays hard, to the very best of his ability, he can be proud of himself even if he loses a competition. However, to me, the object of a competition is to win! *It is not wrong to want to win!*

Spiritually speaking, how you play the "game" of life is important, but winning counts too! And what is your reward? There is a real Heaven to gain . . . and a real hell to shun. Some people don't like to hear that, but it's true. Some don't like hearing that there's a right way to live and a wrong way to live, but that's how the game of life is played.

But it takes more than just a pep talk or a positive message to help you win in the game of life. You have to accept Jesus Christ as your personal Savior to win Heaven and to shun hell. And along the way, you have to walk with Jesus as Lord, and you have to live right.

## Two Battles Man Can't Win on His Own

I ran track in high school, and as a result of my accomplishments, I was later inducted into my high school's Hall of Fame. It took a lot of discipline to win races, but I was compelled to succeed. I would stay after practice and run extra drills, pushing myself to be a better and faster runner. There were many races I won when my body said, "Give up! You can't win!" And my mind said, "Stop! You can't do it!" Sometimes *other people* said I couldn't win against some of my competitors — but I did!

I was successful in those athletic achievements because I worked hard and I was determined. But some battles I cannot win on my own.

It's important to realize that man faces some battles he cannot win by himself — by his own strength, hard work, and determination. Man cannot win spiritual battles by himself. It would be futile for him to attempt to do so.

## The First Battle

The *first* battle man can't win on his own is *to escape a sinful existence.* On his own, man cannot be free from sin, be reconciled to God, and enter Heaven as his eternal dwelling place.

The Bible says, "The things that are impossible with men are possible with God" (Luke 18:27). Christ has translated us from the kingdom of darkness to the Kingdom of light (Col. 1:13). Christ has translated us from the kingdom of defeat to the kingdom of victorious living in Him. It is no longer our destiny to live defeated in life.

What has God done for us in Christ? He has given us a new destiny — a destiny of life eternal, and a destiny of happiness in Christ so that on this earth, we can enjoy "a little bit of Heaven to go to Heaven in!"

While the world is waxing worse and worse, we have a hope. Christ has won eternal victory for us over sin. He won victory for us over death, hell, and the grave. And we can appropriate and enjoy this victory if we will simply believe in and call upon the Name of the Lord. We can escape a sinful existence from the kingdom of darkness and live in the reality of being reconciled with God. We can have peace and joy while the world is in chaos and turmoil.

Jesus said, ". . . My peace I give unto you" (John 14:27). The world cannot understand our peace, because they do not know the Peace-Giver. Many try to find peace in meditation, world religions, and drugs and alcohol. On their own, they cannot find true peace or escape a lifestyle of turmoil and confusion. They need a Savior, Jesus — the Giver of peace.

## The Second Battle

By studying the Old Testament, we find that, historically, God caused people to triumph when they followed Him wholeheartedly. And that is a key for man to win the second battle — *against Satan and his tyranny over the world.* Man must follow God whole-heartedly to win this battle.

In your home or office, you may have a wall filled with trophies and plaques. And you may have a resumé full of outstanding achievements. And it's good to be proud of your accomplishments. But if you're going to triumph, spiritually speaking, you're going to have to follow *God's* orders — *His* instructions. You can't do things your own way, by your own efforts and intellect.

In sports, for example, you can often triumph over a competitor by carefully developing your own winning style — by perfecting every last detail of your style. Then when it comes time to face your opponent, you instinctively do everything just the way you are sup-posed to, and you triumph over the opposition because of your efforts and expertise.

However, when it comes to spiritual battles, you cannot win by using your own style. You have to do things *God's* way.

## 'The Triumph of the Ages'

You see, God is the Triumph of the Ages. In the Old Testament, you'll notice that it was always God who enabled His people to triumph over adversity and foe.

And He often did it against all odds. Ultimately, for God's people to win their battles, they could never forget that God was the Almighty One. And in your spiritual battles, you, too, should remember the great fact that God is Almighty!

No matter what happens in your life, whoever comes or goes, or whatever comes about or *doesn't* come about, God is still Almighty! He is still El Shaddai, the God Who Is More Than Enough. And He will see you through!

The enemy may be accusing you, and threatening and harassing you, telling you that you're not going to triumph over him. But if you will remain calm and keenly aware of the fact that God is Almighty, you will triumph over all opposition. God is God, and He will do what He said He would do! God said He would deliver you and if you will trust Him, He *will* deliver you! He said He would bless you, and He *will* bless you! He said He would see you through — and He *will* do it!

**2 CORINTHIANS 2:14**
**14 Now thanks be unto God, WHICH ALWAYS CAUSETH US TO TRIUMPH IN CHRIST, and**

**maketh manifest the savour of his knowledge by us in every place.**

Let's look at that verse in other translations.

**2 CORINTHIANS 2:14 (*Berkeley*)**
**14 But thanks be to God, who invariably leads us on triumphantly in Christ.**

**2 CORINTHIANS 2:14 (*Williams*)**
**14 . . . He always leads me in His triumphal train, through union with Christ.**

**2 CORINTHIANS 2:14 (*New Jerusalem*)**
**14 Thanks be to God, who always gives us in Christ a part in His triumphal procession.**

**2 CORINTHIANS 2:14 (*New Life*)**
**14 We thank God for the power Christ has given us. He leads us and makes us win in everything.**

I especially like that last translation. "We thank God for the power Christ has given us!" The rest of that verse says, ". . . He leads us and makes us to win in *everything.*" It's not a "hope-so," "maybe-so" proposition. God doesn't make us win in a *few* things — He makes us win in *everything!*

119

## A Way Where There Is No Way

We know that natural man has his limits. We also know that problems and tests can appear so big that it seems there is no way out of them. But God has made a way. That way is through Christ Jesus, our Lord.

There is a place in Christ where we cannot be defeated. It is a place of "no defeat," a place where man is more than a conqueror. Even if failure and defeat are looming ominously on every side and darkness is gaining ground, threatening to overtake you, you have a place of triumph in Christ. Thanks be to God, who *always* causes us to triumph in Christ!

Friend, those aren't my words; they are *God's* words! He didn't promise us *occasional* victory; He *always* causes us to triumph in Christ. We need to take hold of the hand of the Triumphant One, the Triumph of the Ages, and let Him lead us into victory amidst what looks like defeat.

## Your Faith Will See You Through!

Triumphant faith is faith that will take you through the storm, through the test, or through the dark valley of adversity. As you put your faith and trust in the Triumphant One, you may be walking a road that looks black and bleak. But He will lead you out of darkness into the sunshine of victory.

Too many people want to see the entire road ahead before they'll take hold of the Master's hand. But God is saying to them, "Fear not. Walk on, and I will be with you."

If you want to see God's delivering power, you're going to have to walk by faith, one step at a time. It doesn't matter what it looks like or feels like, you will win when you walk with God and have the positive attitude, "My faith will see me through!"

It doesn't matter who you are, this promise of victory and deliverance is for you. Second Corinthians 2:14 was written for people just like you and me, people with natural, human limitations — people who will believe in the Word of God and the promises of God, and who will take hold of those promises in faith.

God said He would take you through all of your trials, and as you look to Him, you will walk out on the other side of those trials victorious! As you believe Him and take hold of His hand, He will lead you through to victory.

God will never turn loose of your hand. It's always man who turns loose of God. But if you don't give up on God, God never gives up on you.

## The Victories of David

Let's look in the book of Psalms again at a man who triumphed again and again because he would not let go of his faith in God.

**PSALM 25:2**

**2  O my God, I trust in thee: let me not be ashamed, let not mine enemies triumph over me.**

The Psalmist David penned this verse. He was well acquainted with adversity, but as we look over the course of his life, we see him triumphant again and again. God caused David to triumph over the lion and the bear when he was just a youth tending his father's sheep (1 Sam. 17:34-36). Later, God gave David a spectacular victory over a giant (vv. 48-51), and he eventually became the king and performed even greater exploits in God.

Before David took office as king, he triumphed repeatedly over King Saul's attempts to kill him. Saul was not a small man; the Bible says he stood head and shoulders over any man in Israel (1 Sam. 9:2; 10:23). At one time, Saul threw a javelin at David at close range, but missed (1 Sam. 18:10,11). God always caused David to triumph as David walked with Him.

## Faith Must Be a Lifestyle

I want to give special attention to a time in David's youth when he experienced a victory that was especially significant to the entire country of Israel. It was a time when God used a boy's faith and five stones fished from a brook to defeat one nation and to save another. I'm talking about David's triumph over Goliath, the Philistine.

You see, it is God that causes us to triumph, but it is our faith in Him that allows Him to do it. It is through our trusting Him that He causes us to win. But we need to learn to trust God *before* we ever reach the battlefield. *We can't wait until we're squaring off with the enemy to learn to receive from God by faith.*

David's faith was a lifestyle. We see it when he prevailed over a lion and bear that tried to destroy his father's sheep. By the time David faced Goliath, he knew what to do. And he knew that his victory was not in his own strength, but in God's.

Goliath had taunted David, telling him, *". . . Come to me, and I will give thy flesh unto the fowls of the air, and to the beasts of the field"* (1 Sam. 17:44). David let him talk. And when Goliath sputtered to a close, David stepped up and told him exactly what *he* was going to do to *him* (vv. 45-47)!

## Empty Boasts

Our enemy, the devil, boasts of himself against us, telling us what he's going to do to us. But, he really hasn't had anything new to say since the beginning — since he was created. Once he said, ". . . *I* will ascend to heaven; *I* will raise my throne above the stars of God . . . . *I* will make myself like the Most High" (Isa. 14:13,14 *NIV*).

But we know what happened to him after that! Isaiah 14:15 says, *"Yet thou shalt be brought down to hell, to the sides of the pit."* Jesus said, *". . . I beheld Satan as lightning fall from heaven"* (Luke 10:18). Yet, since that time, the enemy of our souls has been saying, *"I* this . . ." and *"I* that. . . ."

## Make Your Boast in the Lord!

When Goliath boasted against David, David didn't answer him in his own strength or might. He answered Goliath, *". . . Thou comest to me with a sword, and with a spear, and with a shield: BUT I COME TO THEE IN THE NAME OF THE LORD OF HOSTS, THE GOD OF THE*

*ARMIES OF ISRAEL, whom thou has defied"* (1 Sam. 17:45).

In other words, David boasted in the Lord. He said, in effect, "I don't come as a fighting man, but I come to you in the Name of the Lord God, the God of Israel!"

David had the attitude that His God was more than enough to see him through and give him victory. Then he let go of that sling with one hand — and with one stone, took down the pride of the Philistines.

David realized that he was facing a giant, but he also understood that he was not facing the giant in his own strength or power. It was the power of God flowing through David that caused him to triumph. And in your battles today — whatever it is that you may be facing — it won't be your own power that will cause you to triumph, but the power of God within you that will bring you through to victory.

You may say, "Yes, but you don't know what I'm going through. My situation seems hopeless." Remember that the children of Israel faced situation after situation that seemed impossible. But when they turned to God in covenant, they always came out winners. Well, under the New Covenant, Christians are God's children, too, and the Bible says that our New Covenant is a better covenant (Heb. 8:6)!

"Well, how is God going to do it?" someone asked. "How is He going to deliver me from the mess I'm in?" When your mind, your flesh, and the devil scream out, "No way! It can't happen," let your spirit rise up and talk back! Say, "Not by might, nor by power, but by My Spirit, saith the Lord!" (Zech. 4:6).

Christ has already purchased our victory. Christ has already triumphed over the enemy in His death, burial, and resurrection. The work has already been done. And He did it for you and me.

## Destined for Success

Christ has already defeated Satan. And when we accept Jesus Christ as Savior and Lord, and accept the finished work of the Cross in our lives, His victory becomes our victory. No matter what a negative world might throw our way, we can be victorious.

*The Body of Christ as a whole has not grasped that fact.* We've received *glimpses* of revelation from the Word, and we've moved forward with the truth *to a degree.* But then it seems we allow ourselves to fall back, and we begin to see ourselves as victims instead of victors.

But we have God's Word and His power to triumph over the tyranny of the enemy. *God has designed you to triumph in Christ!* When you become a new creature in Christ, you still live in this world, but you are no longer *of* this world. And this world no longer has any hold on you if you will rise up in Christ and walk in newness of life. Your citizenship is of Heaven, and all the rights and privileges of Heaven belong to you. Through your new birth, you become destined for success throughout eternity. You become free from the tyranny and rule of Satan — from sickness, disease, poverty, bondage, and oppression. Battles you could not win any other way become winnable in Christ.

Friend, it's time to take hold of the truth and press on beyond the limits the world has tried to place on you. It's time to press beyond the limits of your past and live a life beyond limitations.

Someone asked, "How can I do that? If I can't win the battle in my own strength, how do I take hold of the strength of God?'

*By fighting the good fight of faith!*

# Believe, Say, and Do: Three Aspects of the 'Good Fight of Faith'

ten

*If* you are not experiencing triumph over problems and living a life beyond limitations, it's important for you understand that God *wants* to answer your prayers. He wants you to renew your mind with His Word and change your mind for the better, thinking *His* thoughts and walking in *His* ways. He wants you to learn to fight the good fight of faith.

**1 TIMOTHY 6:12 (*NIV*)**
**12 Fight the good fight of the faith. Take hold of the eternal life to which you were called when you made your good confession in the presence of many witnesses.**

Paul wrote this in a letter to Timothy, his son in the faith and fellow minister of the Gospel. By the Spirit of

129

God, he was urging Timothy (and God is urging *us* today) to fight the good fight of faith.

# God Wants You To Learn To Fight!

Notice Paul called it the *good* fight of faith. The fight of faith is a *good* fight because it's a fight we always win! When you walk by faith in God's Word, you are guaranteed to win in life's tests and challenges. Real faith, *Bible* faith, always ends in the realization of victory, leaving defeat and despair far behind.

You might ask, "Well, that sounds too good to be true. Aren't you afraid of giving people too much hope?"

No, I'm not, because *God* said that He would always cause us to triumph in Christ (2 Cor. 2:14), and we know that the just shall live by faith (Hab. 2:4; Rom. 1:17). Therefore, we can fight the good fight of faith and obtain or appropriate the victory that Christ won for us in redemption. God's Word is good *and* it's true! And He holds out hope to us in His Word; we have only to take hold of it.

I didn't say that walking by faith would be easy. I didn't say it wouldn't take some effort on our part. Paul called it the good *fight* of faith. This fight is a part of faith. Too many people want to fight with other people, but the Bible says that our fight is not with flesh and blood (Eph. 6:12). Our fight is to stand our ground against the fear, doubt, and unbelief of Satan and the world, and to *believe, say,* and *do* God's Word so that we will experience victory over life's trials.

As I've just mentioned, the fight of faith involves three basic things: (1) *believing,* (2) *saying,* and (3) *doing.* To walk by faith successfully, you have to *believe, say,* and *do* something. You must *believe* God's Word; *say* God's Word; and *do* God's Word (or *act upon it).*

# Believe

Staying positive in a negative world will require that you continually fight to believe the Word, because the enemy will steal the Word from you if he can. He will come at you through thoughts to try to get you into doubt and unbelief concerning God's Word. In the Garden of Eden, the enemy tempted Eve to disobey God by saying to her, "Has God *really* said that you must not eat of that tree?" (Gen. 3:1).

The enemy can even use other people to steal the Word of God from your heart if you let them. For example, much of modern theology tries to do away with the supernatural, saying, "Those things are not for us today. Those experiences were for a day gone by."

Others will say, "Well, yes, I believe God wants to bless us, but we won't get those blessings till the 'Sweet By-and-By.'"

How sad that these people haven't understood Hebrews 13:8, which says, *"Jesus Christ is the same yesterday and today and forever"* (*NIV*). Friend, you can't get much plainer than that! Jesus Christ is the same Jesus today that He has always been, and He will continue to be the same *forever!*

Then in Malachi 3:6, God said, *"I the Lord do not change"* (*NIV*). God is unchanging, and His Word is unchanging. God's Word is a Rock that we can stand on forever! It will hold us up when nothing else will. To those who believe, God's Word is His power unto salvation (Rom. 1:16).

We will have to fight the good fight to hold on to what we believe. To do that, we will need to feed and meditate upon the Word of God continually until it is so strong in us that nothing can move us from it; no one can talk us out of it. No circumstance can shake us, because we're holding on to the Rock eternal, Jesus Christ, the Living Word of God!

## Seeing as God Sees

Over the years, I've heard my dad say many times to those to whom he ministered healing, "See yourself well. See yourself doing what you couldn't do before."

For example, if you're a minister of the Gospel and you're facing a challenge in your body, see yourself well, ministering to others. If you're an evangelist, see yourself preaching to thousands and winning multitudes to Christ.

If you're a school teacher, see yourself as a gifted teacher. If you're in the medical profession, see yourself caring for patients with great skill and compassion.

I think every athlete who has ever become a success on a professional level has seen himself or herself as a success in advance. For example, a football player might see himself catching winning passes. A basketball player might see himself scoring winning points with just seconds left in the game.

Similarly, as we take hold of God's Word with our heart, we should begin to see ourselves with the manifestation of that Word in our lives. We should envision our answer coming to pass. With the eyes of our spirit, we should see it as done.

You may not have a penny to your name, but when the revelation of divine prosperity dawns on you, you will see yourself with plenty of money to meet your needs and the needs of others. You will see yourself with money in your pocket.

I'm not talking about just positive thinking or mental power. I'm talking about believing in the power of God's Word! I'm talking about being fully persuaded that what He promised, He is able also to perform (Rom. 4:21). Jesus said, *". . . If thou canst believe, all things are possible to him that believeth"* (Mark 9:23).

Our minds — our natural human reasoning — will fight us every step of the way as we fight to believe everything that Christ did for us in His death, burial, and resurrection. Many have not fully grasped the realities of redemption. How do I know that? Because if they fully grasped the truth of what God did for them in Christ, they would be appropriating and experiencing more of His blessings and benefits. They would be living life beyond limitations.

## The 'Rest' of Faith

We know that in the midst of a world of negativism and despair, we sometimes find ourselves facing some hard work. Well, a fight is a struggle, isn't it? And the

Bible talks about *laboring* to enter into the "rest" of faith (Heb. 4:11).

What is the "rest" of faith? When you're walking by faith, you have peace in your heart as you rest upon the promises of God. You are fully persuaded that what God promised, He is able and willing to perform (Rom. 4:21). You can rest, because you know the final outcome. You have "inside information" –– information inside God's holy Word! You are assured that God is at work in your situation and in your life, and there is a peacefulness about you that passes human understanding (Phil. 4:7).

In fact, others will wonder how you're able to have such peace and joy in the midst of your storm. It's because you're fighting the good fight of faith — you're laboring to *believe*, *say*, and *do* the Word of God, and you're entering into the "rest" of faith.

## Say

The second aspect of the good fight of faith is *saying*. We must fight to continually say what the Word says instead of talking about our problems and circumstances. Some people will try to tell you, "It's not right to confess the Bible. That's not traditional Christianity."

135

But there isn't anything more traditional in Christianity than saying what the Bible says! If you're a Christian, you had to believe and say what the Bible says so that you could be saved. You had to believe in your heart that God raised Jesus from the dead, and you had to confess, or say, that Jesus is Lord (Rom. 10:9). So you see, Bible-based confession *is* traditional Christianity. In fact, Christianity has often been called The Great Confession.

The Bible is God's Word, and God and His Word are one. The Bible is God speaking to us. We need to continually say what God says. We will experience great victories in life if we do.

## Where God's Word Is Concerned, Do Not Keep Quiet!

*You should never face the enemy, your trials, or your problems with your mouth shut!* Instead, you should confront them and maintain the bold confession, "I am the righteousness of God in Christ" (2 Cor. 5:21)! "By Jesus' stripes, I was and am healed" (Isa. 53:5; 1 Peter 2:24)! "God meets all of my needs according to His riches in glory by Christ Jesus" (Phil. 4:19)! "I am more than a conqueror through Him who loved me and gave Himself for me" (Rom. 8:37)! "By the blood of the Lamb, the Lord Jesus Christ, I overcome" (Rev. 12:11)!

It's important not only to say what the Bible says, but also to *maintain* your confession. No matter what the obstacle, test, or trial, it's vital to maintain your confession! And no matter who tells you to stop confessing God's Word, do not keep quiet!

If blind Bartimaeus had been quiet as he sat there by the road where Jesus was passing, he would not have received his sight. But he cried out, "Jesus! Have mercy on me!"

Others said, "Be quiet!" But Bartimaeus cried even louder, "Jesus! Have mercy on me!" When others tried to make Bartimaeus stop speaking, he proclaimed, "Jesus is my answer! And I will not be denied" (Mark 10:46-52)!

The pattern of "believing and saying" is not man's idea. This is God's pattern; it's how he created the world to begin with (Heb. 11:3). God said, "Let there be . . . " and there was (Gen. 1:3-28)!

The Bible says we are created in the likeness of God and that we should imitate Him "as dear children" (Gen. 1:26; Eph. 5:1). Therefore, we should imitate this pattern of believing and saying in our own lives. Does God believe His own words? Yes! God believes that what He says will come to pass. So what should *we* believe and say? *Exactly what God says in His Word.*

## Jesus — The Will of God in Action

In His earth walk, Jesus was the will of God in action. He said, "He that has seen Me has seen the Father" (John 14:9). And Jesus demonstrated this same pattern of believing and saying.

**MARK 11:12-14,20-23**

**12 And on the morrow, when they were come from Bethany, he [Jesus] was hungry:**

**13 And seeing a fig tree afar off having leaves, he came, if haply he might find any thing thereon: and when he came to it, he found nothing but leaves; for the time of figs was not yet.**

**14 And Jesus answered and said unto it, No man eat fruit of thee hereafter for ever. And his disciples heard it.**

**20 And in the morning, as they passed by, they saw the fig tree dried up from the roots.**

**21 And Peter calling to remembrance saith unto him, Master, behold, the fig tree which thou cursedst is withered away.**

**22 And Jesus answering saith unto them, Have faith in God.**

**23 For verily I say unto you, that whosoever shall SAY unto this mountain, be thou removed, and be thou cast into the sea; and shall not doubt in his heart, but shall believe that those things which he SAITH shall come to pass; he shall have whatsoever he SAITH.**

You see, these verses show that our God uses the same spiritual principle — to believe and say. And the man and woman of God should do the same to not limit God in their lives.

Notice in Mark 11:23 that some form of the word "say" is found three times in connection with Jesus' teaching, and the word "believe" is there only once. That tells me that we need to emphasize the *saying* part of the good fight of faith.

Regarding Mark 11:23, the Lord once told my father, Kenneth E. Hagin, "You'll have to do three times as much teaching on the saying part as on the believing part." We need to continually speak or *say* what we believe concerning God's Word.

Do you have any mountains in your way? If you do, talk to them! Tell them to get out of your way!

Someone said, "But I don't feel worthy to speak to the mountain like Jesus did. He's the Son of God. I've made so many mistakes in life."

Listen, friend, no matter how many mistakes you have made or how you have disobeyed God in the past, God is good and rich in mercy to all who call upon Him in sincerity (Ps. 86:5; Rom. 10:12)! You *can* fight the good fight of faith, and you *can* win victories in the midst of life's trials . . . no matter what! You won't be defeated if you will not quit — if you won't quit *believing* and *saying*!

Believing and speaking God's Word will lift you out of negativism and defeat and set you on the path to victory. It will strengthen your spirit, renew your mind, and give you a new, positive attitude of faith and victory.

## Do

The third aspect of the good fight of faith is *doing*. Some people are confused about what it means to act on the Word of God. Simply translated, it means to act like the Bible is so — because it is!

What would you do if the battle you are facing were already won — if you saw the answer manifest before

140

your very eyes? How would you act? Well, by way of illustration, suppose you were appearing on a television game show. Then suppose you won it all — thousands and thousands of dollars, plus a grand-prize package!

You would get a little excited, wouldn't you? You would probably jump and scream and act very happy. You would probably hug the game show host. Then all your family members in the audience would run up and congratulate you, and everyone would be jumping up and down, hugging one another, and shouting!

Well, through Christ, we have won much more than money and prizes. We have won eternal life! We have won fellowship and companionship with the Father and His Son the Savior. We've won help in time of need. We've won health and prosperity!

## Our 'Rod' of Authority

In the Book of Exodus, we can read about the great host of God's people fleeing Egypt's bondage under the leadership of Moses. Helpless and distressed as slaves to Pharaoh and the Egyptians, they were supernaturally delivered from Egypt by the hand of God.

After the ten curses that plagued Egypt, including the death of all of Egypt's firstborn, Pharaoh finally set God's chosen people free. But then they came to the Red Sea.

After he let the Israelite slaves go free, Pharaoh's heart became hardened once again, and he and his army took off in pursuit of the newly freed Israelites. With the sea in front of them and the Egyptians in heavy pursuit, the children of Israel literally had nowhere to go.

Moses cried out to God on behalf of the people, and God answered, "Why are you crying to Me? Tell the people to *go forward!*"

Then God told Moses, "Stretch forth thy rod over the sea and divide it."

Moses did as God said, the sea parted, and the children of Israel passed through on dry ground (Exod. 14:5-31)!

Have you ever been in a situation in which you felt like you were "between a rock and a hard place"? Moses found himself in that position. He cried out to God to do something, and God replied to Moses, in effect, "*You* do something!"

You may be between the "enemy and the sea" in whatever you're facing. God is saying to you, "Stretch forth thy rod and go forward!"

Moses' rod was a symbol of God's spoken Word. Today, the rod is our speaking forth the revelation of God's Word that's in our heart. We don't have a literal rod to stretch out over our problem, but we do have the Word of God. We don't have a rod in our hand, but we do have the Word in our mouth.

**ROMANS 10:8**

**8 But what saith it? The word is nigh thee, even in thy mouth and in thy heart: that is, the word of faith, which we preach.**

Moses' rod was a rod of authority. And we as believers have been given spiritual authority. The Lord Jesus Christ gave us our authority (Luke 10:19). We have been authorized to use His Name and His Word of power over all the power of the enemy! We have commanding power over what the enemy tries to do in our lives.

Yet many people will whine and cry, "I need someone to pray for me. The devil has been after me."

But the Bible doesn't say you should have someone else pray that the devil will stop attacking you. It says, ". . . *Resist the devil, and he will flee from you*" (James 4:7). In other words, "*You* resist the devil." That word "flee" means *to run from, as in terror.*

We don't have to live our life "down and out." Jesus won the victory, and He won the ability for us to say in the midst of every trial, "Thanks be to God who *always* give me the victory!"

# A Personal Story

When I was fifteen years old, I contracted an ear disease. At that time, it was an incurable fungus that my doctor said migrated to the States with some soldiers who had been stationed in the South Sea Islands. He said I would have to live with the condition for the rest of my life and that it would eventually destroy the hearing in my left ear. He also said I should never put my head under water again and that it would be better if we moved to Arizona or to the California desert where the climate was dry. That would hinder the growth of the fungus and prolong the number of years I'd have hearing in that ear.

The disease caused so much pain that at times, I couldn't sleep at night. Or if I was asleep and happened to touch my left ear, I'd bolt upright in bed, screaming in pain. There were times when the ear became swollen to twice its size.

Up until that time in my life, my dad had always received healing for me when sickness tried to come against me. I'd been instantly healed of sicknesses many times. But this time, his faith didn't work for me, and the Lord told him it was time for me to start doing my

144

own praying and believing. So I prayed to receive healing of the ear disease.

When I returned to school after the Christmas break
that year, as I was getting ready for P.E. class, I had my
mind set on my healing! That day, I had said, "This is
my day!" I could hardly wait to get out of math class. I
shoved my books into my locker and took off for the
gym with bold determination.

Our school had an Olympic-sized pool, and the P.E.
classes took turns using it. I knew our class was going
to swim that day. I burst through the double doors of
the locker room, and they both swung open so wide,
one of the doors hit the teacher! He said, "Hagin, what
in the world is the matter with you?"

"Never mind, Coach," I answered and continued
toward my locker. I put on my swimming trunks and,
with the same determination and fervor, burst into the
pool area. I jumped into the pool and swam down to
the bottom. Then I swam underwater toward the other
end of the pool. With every stroke, my mind was
screaming at me, "You're crazy! Don't you remember
what that doctor said? You're going to go deaf for sure!"

But my heart was telling a different story. With great
confidence and joy, I said in my heart, "I believe I
receive my healing. My God is able! I'm healed!"

When I reached the other side, I pushed off from the bottom and headed for the top of the pool. When my head broke that water, I heard a loud clap inside my head, and I screamed, "Thank God, I'm healed!"

From that day to this one, I've been healed of that fungus! And instead of losing hearing in my left ear, my hearing in that ear became better than in my right ear! I spent three years in the United States Army, and when I entered the military, my ears were tested. I ended up in communications, where we used Morse code and other devices which required that the equipment operators have perfect hearing.

## *Believe, Say,* and *Do* — A Winning Combination

What would have happened if I'd never acted on what I believed? The power of God met me at my point of believing with all my heart that healing was mine and that I had already received my answer. I was determined to see it come to pass! But I couldn't just sit back and take the attitude, "I'll just wait for God to do something; then I'll *know* I'm healed."

Don't take the attitude that you're going to wait until you see your answer before you start believing. Start believing *right now* that God's Word is true! Start saying right now, "In Christ, I'm a winner." Start acting victorious, because that's how God sees you — a winner!

The devil will try to keep you in the arena of the senses and of human reasoning. He will even try to accuse you of past mistakes and wrongdoing to try to condemn you and weaken your faith.

You're going to have to stand your ground against him. You're going to have to fight to believe God's Word and to hold on to your beliefs. You're going to have to fight to say continually what the Word says. In the midst of adversity and turmoil, you're going to have to shout! You're going to have to say, "Yes, Satan, I know what I did. But I've been forgiven! Christ has delivered me! I'm free! And I'm going to *stay* free in the Name of Jesus!"

God is a God of victory and triumph. And God is good all the time. He has designed you for success. He created you to triumph over trials and live life beyond limitations. He created you to live in a positive environment.

"But I don't *feel* very victorious," you might say.

Thank God, you don't have to rely on feelings to know whether or not you're victorious. You can determine in your heart: "God said it. I believe it. And that settles it!" You can rely on the faithfulness of God and His love for you. You can say with Paul, "Nothing can separate me from the love of my limitless God" (Rom. 8:39) and "I can *do* all things through Christ which strengtheneth me" (Phil. 4:13)! You can *"believe, say, and do"* your way to victory!

# Victory Runs on Two Rails

## eleven

*Finally,* brethren, whatsoever things are true, whatsoever things are honest, whatsoever things are just, whatsoever things are pure, whatsoever things are lovely, whatsoever things are of good report; if there by any virtue, and if there be any praise, think on these things. Those things, which ye have both learned, and received, and heard, and seen in me, do: and the God of peace shall be with you.

— Philippians 4:8,9

Throughout this book, I've shared practical, scriptural methods by which we can keep a positive attitude in a negative world. We've looked in-depth at two primary ways we can stay positive in the midst of trouble and adversity: (1) through *prayer* and (2) through *renewing your mind.*

My final point to remaining positive in a negative world is *to value others and walk in the light of love.* We must recognize the best in others instead of scrutinizing them and looking for the worst.

You simply can't stay positive if you're not thinking on things that are "pure, true, and lovely" as we read in Philippians 4:8 — and that includes thinking on things that are pure, true, and lovely about other people.

Let's look at that verse in *The Living Bible.*

**PHILIPPIANS 4:8 (*TLB*)**
**8  . . . Fix your thoughts on what is true and good and right. Think about things that are pure and lovely, and dwell on the fine, good things in others. Think about all you can praise God for and be glad about.**

People are not perfect, and we won't be until we leave this world for Heaven. *But we are constantly being perfected.* We are constantly striving in that direction as we give our attention to the Word and prayer and to fellowship with God and with others of like, precious faith.

When we give our attention to the Word, it's important that we give our attention to the *entire* Word of God, not just parts of it. For example, the Bible says,

*"Not forsaking the assembling of ourselves together, as the manner of some is; but exhorting one another: and so much the more, as ye see the day approaching"* (Heb. 10:25). Yet how many Christians have you heard say, in effect, "I don't need to go to church. I can get just as much from the preacher on TV." These same Christians often justify their position by saying they've tried different churches but weren't happy with the pastors or the church people.

Friend, pastors aren't perfect either! And if they were, they would have no church to pastor, because churches aren't perfect either! I'm not trying to make excuses for people's imperfections, but I am trying to convey that we should be constantly striving for perfection in God, and at the same time, we should realize that others are doing the same.

It's been said that our Christian walk, like a train, runs on two rails: faith and love. Without strong love, there can be no strong faith. You show me a person who is strong in faith, and I'll show you a person who is strong in love. The opposite is also true: You show me a person who is strong in love, and I'll show you a person who is strong in faith. Faith and love go together; they work hand in hand.

**GALATIANS 5:6**

**6  For in Jesus Christ neither circumcision availeth any thing, nor uncircumcision; but faith which worketh by love.**

Many have called my father the modern-day "father of faith." Yes, he is a man of strong faith. But if you know him, you know that his strong faith walk comes from his strong love walk. If you were to follow his life, you would find that he never says anything bad about anyone. He has always said to me, "Anyone can dwell on the negative, but it takes someone with backbone to dwell on the positive."

Now why did he say that? Because, if we're going to go with the positive, we're going to go upstream against the crowd. For example, you might have to go against the crowd that's putting someone else down. You might have to befriend someone who's been picked on and abused. But that is love's way.

## Focus On the Positive in Others

My father taught me to always look for the good in others. We can always find something positive in others if we look for it. For example, some people have an especially good reputation as being truthful and honest (and we all should have that kind of reputation). Others have a reputation for being especially diligent and faithful. Those are examples of positive qualities we should look for instead of focusing on the negative.

One way to keep a positive attitude toward the faults and imperfections of others is to pray for them! The Apostle Paul practiced this, and so should we.

**PHILIPPIANS 1:3-5 (*NIV*)**
**3  I thank my God every time I remember you.**
**4  In all my prayers for all of you, I always pray with joy**
**5  because of your partnership in the gospel from the first day until now.**

I want you to notice that even though the Philippians weren't perfect — they weren't doing everything exactly right — Paul said, "I thank my God every time I remember you." Every time he thought about them, what did he remember about them? He remembered that they were his partners in the Gospel.

If every time a certain person comes to your mind, you think something negative about him or her, you need to change what you're thinking. You need to renew your mind to think something positive about that person.

153

Find something positive — admirable or praiseworthy — and then think on that when he or she comes to mind. Consistently doing that will change your outlook on life.

You might be saying, "How could Paul thank God for and think good things about *everyone* he remembered in the Philippian church?"

First, because Paul was a person of prayer and the Word. We can look at his life and see that's how he had stayed positive in a negative world. Second, Paul *chose* to thank God for those people and to pray for them. We have a choice about what we think or say when we remember others.

As a pastor, after I've counseled someone through a problem or crisis, I refuse to think anything negative about that person when I see him or her again. After receiving counseling, certain people in my church have said to me, "I feel so embarrassed about what I spoke to you about." I pastor a church of more than five thousand members, so if some length of time has passed, I sometimes genuinely don't even remember what it was we talked about! At other times, I have a vague recollection. But I am just glad to have pointed them to Jesus and to the Word and helped them through to victory.

I can't afford to hold in my mind all the negative things I hear, so I refuse to think about those things. I put them out of my mind and replace them with things that are positive — pure, true, and lovely.

## If We're Going to Hold Out Hope to the Lost, We Must Remain Positive

As Christians, we need to be busy about our Father's business and concentrate on the fields of harvest rather than the faults of others. Paul practiced this and exhorted us to do the same.

**PHILIPPIANS 4:9 (*NIV*)**

**9  Whatever you have learned or received or heard from me, or seen in me — put it into practice. And the God of peace will be with you.**

Daily we must put into practice the things that will keep us positive in a negative world. We must let our light shine and hold out hope to the lost and dying and to those who are hurting. The people of God — the Body of Christ — are the only light the unsaved have in this world. So let's be a positive influence in their lives.

We are not to hide our heads in the sand and ignore everything that is negative. But in the midst of nega- tivism and despair, we can stay positive with the power of God in operation in our lives. We can overcome the *negative* with the *positive* and receive the blessings and benefits of God by thinking and acting positively — in line with His Word.

# Hope, Help, and Healing

If you haven't already done so, I encourage you to step out of negativism and defeat. Make prayer, the Word, and walking in the light of God's love your first priorities. We need to demonstrate the love and power of God to a world that is full of evil and hate. We need to walk in love toward our fellow man, especially toward those who are of the household of faith (Gal. 6:10).

If we are not walking in the light of love, our faith will not work, because faith works by love (Gal. 5:6). Our prayers will be ineffective because we are harboring wrong attitudes in our heart.

I've heard this comment frequently over the years, "Well, I would forgive and walk in love, but you just don't know how badly I've been hurt."

No, I don't, but Jesus does. The Bible says that He is touched by the *feelings* of our infirmities or weaknesses (Heb. 4:15). And no matter how badly you've been wronged — no matter what anyone has or has not done — Jesus still loves and cares about you. If you will focus on what *He* thinks about you instead of how wrongly you've been treated, you will be on your way to hope, help, and healing.

We've all been hurt by others at some time or another. No, it doesn't feel good, but you don't have to dwell on bad feelings and the wrong actions of others. You can't control what others say and do, but you can control *you!* You can decide that you're going to walk in love no matter what, and you can refuse to become negative.

Many don't realize that holding a grudge against someone else does not hurt that other person as much as it hurts them. If you become bitter and unforgiving, you're going to become negative in your attitude. You will not only stop the power of God from operating in your life, but you will also give place to the devil. You will allow the him to take advantage of you.

Let this be your heartfelt confession: "I choose to stay positive in a negative world. I refuse to allow negative reports to dwell in my mind. I will think on things that are positive — pure, true, lovely, admirable, and praiseworthy. I will walk in the light of God's love and receive and enjoy the blessings of God in my life. Then I can hold out hope to others so that they, too, may receive His blessings."

# The Best Is Yet To Come!

## twelve

*In* the midst of great battles, great victory waits just around the corner for those who will stand fearlessly on God's Word, refusing to give up. Great blessings will fall on the believing ones who know the secret of staying positive when the world says they should be negative. The Bible says, *"Eye hath not seen, nor ear heard, neither have entered into the heart of man, the things which God hath prepared for them that love him"* (1 Cor. 2:9).

In other words, the best is yet to come!

You may have enjoyed some good results from prayer and from the Word, but as you continue walking with God, the best is yet to come!

What we do with the Word of God and His promises will determine our future. Will we hold to the Word of God as something dear? Will we allow ourselves to

159

become negative in a negative world? Or will we remain positive, allowing God to deliver us from trouble and receive glory from our lives? With all the unrest going on in the world, we don't know exactly what tomorrow will hold. But we do know who holds our tomorrows!

## Crossing the Finish Line of Faith

*Real faith will always end in victory.* But how many people start out believing God for something, and then "fizzle out" when the road ahead seems too long or too dark. Have you ever heard a teacher or employer say about someone, "He has great potential, but he never finishes what he starts."

Don't ever let that be said about you! Don't be someone who starts out by faith, but doesn't endure in the hard places. If you do, you'll never get to the place in life where God wants you.

Many people look at my mom and dad, Oretha and Kenneth E. Hagin, and think they were always as prosperous as they are today. But at one time, when I was a kid, we didn't even have a car! And for years, I slept on a rollaway bed that I put wherever I could find a place to sleep — from the kitchen to the screened-in porch!

More than once, we went to church hungry, with no food in the pantry. But my dad kept preaching that Jesus is the Provider.

There were times it certainly looked as if God wasn't meeting our needs. But Dad always told us, "God is our source, and He will meet our needs. If we'll be faithful, He will provide." And He always did.

I can still hear my father's voice as he'd tell me when I was just a young man, "Son, with God, payday is not every Friday. But if you'll learn to stay steady and endure in the hard spots, you will reap the rewards of victory. Payday will come!"

That's why it's important not to judge a person by where he is in life today. His life is not over yet, if he is walking with God, the best is yet to come!

## Blessed in the Here and the Hereafter

Not only can the Christian look for better days to come as he puts God's Word to work in the midst of his tests, trials, and temptations, but he can look forward to Heaven as his eternal home. For the Christian, the best is always yet to come, even when he passes from this life!

I once heard an interesting story about a dear saint who was preparing to die, as she knew it was time for her to go be with the Lord. She called for her pastor, and they discussed the details of her funeral service. As he started out the door to leave, she said, "Wait a minute, Pastor. There's something else."

"What that?" came the pastor's reply.

"This is very important," the woman continued. "I want to be buried with a fork in my right hand."

The pastor stood looking at the woman, not knowing quite what to say.

"That surprises you, doesn't it?" the woman asked.

"Well, to be honest, I'm puzzled by the request," explained the pastor.

The woman explained. "In all my years of attending church socials and pot-luck dinners, I always remember that when the dishes of the main course were being cleared, someone would inevitably lean over and say, 'Keep your fork.'

"It was my favorite part because I knew that something better was coming, like velvety chocolate cake or deep-dish apple pie. Something wonderful, and with substance!

"So, I just want people to see me there in that casket with a fork in my hand and I want them to wonder, 'What's with the fork?'

"Then I want you to tell them: 'Keep your fork! The best is yet to come!'"

Your life may be going great right now, but you can rejoice that the best is yet to come! You have more to look forward to in this life, and you have the glad hope, the promise of Heaven.

Or your life may be a dark trial today — your "midnight hour" — but you, too, can rejoice, because the best is yet to come! God will deliver you as you take hold of His Word and His strength and, by faith, stand your ground against that trial.

We can thank God for all He has done for us — for our salvation, for the Holy Ghost, for all our material blessings, and for all the joys of life. But our best days are still ahead — when we will see the face of God and rejoice around His throne. That blessed hope alone is cause enough for us to rejoice. But we can rejoice today for *all* of our tomorrows, knowing that the best is yet to come!

# About the Author

Rev. Kenneth Hagin Jr., president of Kenneth Hagin Ministries and pastor of RHEMA Bible Church, seizes every ministry opportunity to impart the attitude of "I cannot be defeated, and I will not quit." He has ministered for almost 50 years, beginning as an associate pastor and traveling evangelist. He has organized and developed 14 RHEMA Bible Training Centers around the world and is the founding pastor of RHEMA Bible Church. With his wife, Rev. Lynette Hagin, Rev. Hagin Jr. co-hosts *Rhema for Today*, a weekday radio program broadcast throughout the United States, and *RHEMA Praise*, a weekly television broadcast.

To fulfill the urgent call of God to prepare the Church for a deeper experience of His Presence, Rev. Hagin Jr. emphasizes key spiritual truths about faith, healing, and other vital subjects. He often ministers with a strong healing anointing, and his ministry helps lead believers into a greater experience of the glory of God.

# God has a *specific* plan for your life.
## *Are you ready?*

# RHEMA Bible Training Center

"... Giving all *diligence*, add to your faith *virtue*, to virtue *knowledge* ....
For if these things are yours and *abound*, you will be neither barren nor *unfruitful* in the knowledge of our Lord Jesus Christ."

—2 Peter 1:5,8 (*NKJV*)

- Take your place in the Body of Christ for the last great revival.

- Learn to rightly divide God's Word and hear His voice clearly.

- Discover how to be a willing vessel for God's glory.

- Receive practical, hands-on ministry training from experienced ministers.

*Qualified instructors are waiting to teach, train, and help you fulfill your destiny!*

**Call today for information or application material.**
1-888 28-FAITH (1-888-283-2484)—Offer #P743

## www.rbtc.org

*RHEMA Bible Training Center admits students of any race, color, or ethnic origin.*